Emerson and Thoreau:

TRANSCENDENTALISTS

IN CONFLICT

Emerson and Thoreau:

TRANSCENDENTALISTS

IN CONFLICT

By

JOEL PORTE

Wesleyan University Press

MIDDLETOWN, CONNECTICUT

Library of Congress Catalog Card Number: 66–14662
Manufactured in the United States of America
First Edition

For my wife Ilana d'Ancona Porte

Contents

Preface

WHILE attempting to explain the hidden meaning of the book of Genesis in his *Confessions,* St. Augustine managed to describe perfectly the major fear of every future critic, literary or biblical, when he anticipated the eternal objection to every individual interpretive effort, including his own: " 'Moses did not mean what you say. He meant what I say.' " The only solution to the problem, St. Augustine wisely concluded, is that no one reading of anything exhausts the matter: Moses meant all that we can possibly dream of, and more. Perhaps this is finally to say that only that literature is worth studying which provides us with the richest opportunities for examining our own minds.

More to the point, what I offer in the following pages is, to borrow Charles Feidelson's term, most emphatically only one "version" of Emerson and Thoreau. It is, I should add, a version of both writers in which I hope all students of the subject will find some validity. But I shall consider my purpose achieved if I can at least succeed in effecting a refocus of interest in the Emerson-Thoreau relationship, without necessarily succeeding in proving that my version of Emerson and Thoreau is the "true" one. Indeed, no single study of such complex major figures—especially one that attempts to deal with them both—can make any claim to comprehensiveness; limitation, I take it, being the necessary guarantee of both virtue and vice in a single point of view. The large body of criticism that has grown up around Emerson and Thoreau in our own time sufficiently attests both to the difficulty of dealing with them definitively and to the fascination of trying. The only truly comprehensive criticism is simply the sum total of all the individual studies in depth from which we have learned and will continue to learn so much: to mention just a few names, those of Mark Van Doren, F. O. Matthiessen, Stephen Whicher, Sherman Paul, Charles Feidelson and Perry Miller.

I have attempted here to recreate what I believe to have been the genuinely dialectical nature of the relationship between Emerson and Thoreau; essentially, I have tried to document a lack of agreement. I would be the first to insist, however, that there is more to be said about the relationship between Emerson and Thoreau than is embodied in my own formulation. But I am relieved of any great anxiety on this score because of the number and excellence of studies, such as those I have mentioned, that take another point of view. I do hope, nevertheless, that what is lost to comprehensiveness in my own approach is gained in speculative interest.

Among my many obligations, I want especially to mention my indebtedness to the late Perry Miller, whose thorough scrutiny of an earlier version of this study helped me to many clarifications and to the correcting of many faults. I owe thanks also to Professor Kenneth S. Lynn for much good advice and needed encouragement. And I am grateful to my friend Llewellyn Howland III for his unflagging interest in this work. The manuscript profited immeasurably from the criticisms, at once sympathetic and sharp, of Alan Levensohn, as well as from those of Professor George R. Creeger of Wesleyan University. The generosity of the Henry P. Kendall

Foundation aided the preparation of the manuscript for the press.

To those good and true friends—Barbara Charlesworth Gelpi, Albert Gelpi, and Robert Kiely—whose wisdom and affection I have depended on for so long, I can only record, but never adequately express, my gratitude.

J. P.

Cambridge, Massachusetts
June 1965

Abbreviations

For convenience, the following abbreviations are used:

C *The Complete Works of Ralph Waldo Emerson*, Centenary Edition. 12 vols. Boston and New York, 1903–04.

J *The Journals of Ralph Waldo Emerson*, ed. Edward Waldo Emerson and Waldo Emerson Forbes. 10 vols. Boston and New York, 1909–14.

Jn *The Journals and Miscellaneous Notebooks of Ralph Waldo Emerson*, ed. William H. Gilman, Alfred R. Ferguson, George P. Clark, and Merrell R. Davis. Volume 1. Cambridge: Harvard University Press, 1960.

W *The Writings of Henry David Thoreau*, Walden Edition. 20 vols. Boston and New York, 1906.

Thoreau's *A Week on the Concord and Merrimack Rivers* is shortened throughout to *A Week*.

Emerson and Thoreau:

TRANSCENDENTALISTS

IN CONFLICT

Introduction

. . . there has sprung up in Boston a sect of philosophers
known as Transcendentalists. On inquiring what this appella-
tion might be supposed to signify, I was given to understand
that whatever was unintelligible would be certainly transcendental.

Dickens, *American Notes*

*   *   *

He is a German by birth, and is called Giant Transcendentalist; but as to his form, his features, his substance,
and his nature generally, it is the chief peculiarity of this huge
miscreant that neither he for himself, nor anybody for him, has
ever been able to describe them.

Hawthorne, "The Celestial Railroad"

*   *   *

Yesterday I dined with Mr Horace Greeley & Mr Brisbane, the
socialist, at a Graham Boarding House. Mr Brisbane promised
me a full exposition of the principles of Fourierism & Association, as soon as I am once lodged at the Globe Hotel. Il faut
soumettre: Yet I foresaw in the moment when I encountered
these two new friends here, that I cannot content them. They
are bent on popular action: I am in all my theory, ethics, &
politics a poet and of no more use in their New York than a

rainbow or a firefly. Meantime they fasten me in their thought to "Transcendentalism," whereof you know I am wholly guilt-less, and which is spoken of as a known & fixed element like salt or meal: So that I have to begin by endless disclaimers & explanations—'I am not the man you take me for.'

Emerson, Letter to Lidian Emerson,
March 1, 1842

*   *   *

The fact is I am a mystic, a transcendentalist, and a natural philosopher to boot. Now I think of it, I should have told them at once that I was a transcendentalist. That would have been the shortest way of telling them that they would not under-stand my explanations.

Thoreau, *Journal*, March 5, 1853

*   *   *

MOST Emerson-Thoreau criticism in our time has tended to follow Mark Van Doren in his statements, made in 1916, that "Thoreau is a specific Emerson" and that Thoreau's philo-sophical position was "almost identical with Emerson's." [1] This essay might be considered an attempt to modify Professor Van Doren's dictum through a re-examination of the relationship between the two men.

Any such attempt must deal with the vexing question of Transcendentalism, the difficulties of which are succinctly suggested by the four quotations placed as epigraphs to this introduction. Fortunately, however, besides warning us of dangers, the four statements also offer a foothold for further exploration.

In the first place, all the statements agree in stating quite explicitly that one needs circumspection in dealing with Tran-scendentalism: *caveat emptor!* It was for Emerson simply not "a known & fixed element"; for Hawthorne, maddeningly inde-scribable; for Dickens, comically unintelligible; and for Thoreau, happily inexplicable. Hawthorne insinuates a suggestion of European origin and irreligion ("miscreant"). Dickens is content to consider it simply another Boston peculiarity (after a mention of Carlyle, he goes on to rest Transcendentalism squarely on Emerson's shoulders). Greeley and Brisbane, according to Emerson's letter, apparently expected every Transcendentalist to be at least a potential reformer. If *that* was what they understood by the term, Emerson would have no part of it, for he here describes himself as a poet—an impractical man, unused to the world of action. At all events, his closing remark—"I am not the man you take me for"—might be used as a kind of Emersonian motto, suggesting the now familiar difficulty of defining Emerson's position: his true self would always be elusive, perhaps even to Emerson. On his side, Thoreau could consider himself, as a Transcendentalist, both a mystic and a naturalist—his very self-definition characteristically a paradox. He would glory in being, as a Transcendentalist, a very special species of a genus hard enough to describe in the first place.

Taken together, these four statements more or less define the problems that any discussion of American Transcendentalism has had to deal with: its nature, a confusing conglomeration of disparate beliefs and practices; its origins (German, English, indigenous, or something else); whether it was essentially religious or anti-religious in character; whether Emerson or someone else was its true spokesman; its relation to reform movements, particularly such things as utopian communities, abolition, and temperance; whether it advocated society or solitude, action or reflection, art or life; and, finally, its attitude toward nature—mystical or scientific, idealistic or naturalistic. All of these matters have been discussed in attempts to define Transcendentalism, and some of them will be of central importance to our investigation of the relationship between Emerson and Thoreau.

What is especially interesting, however, about Emerson's letter to his wife is his disingenuous insistence on being "wholly guiltless" of Transcendentalism. For if Emerson believed that at the time, he was apparently alone in his belief. Dickens' statement attributing Transcendentalism to Emerson also dates from 1842. And Hawthorne, in the original version of "The Hall of Fantasy," published in February 1843 (three months before "The Celestial Railroad"; both were reprinted in *Mosses from an Old Manse* [1846]), showed Emerson surrounded by "all manner of Transcendentalists and disciples of the Newness, most of whom betrayed the power of his intellect by its modifying influence upon their own." [2] Emerson's vital connection with Transcendentalism was obviously assumed in Boston, at least in 1842, and there was good reason for this assumption. In January 1842, just two months before writing the letter to Lidian quoted above, Emerson had delivered his lecture "The Transcendentalist" at the Masonic Temple there.

Although the lecture glows with sympathy for the errant youths who had given themselves heart and soul to the "new views," Emerson was careful to create the impression that he might have been speaking only as an observer. He called the Transcendentalists "children" (C, I, 348), apologized for their withdrawal from the world of action, and suggested that they would return one day. He conceded the dangers of Transcendentalism by warning that "there will be cant and pretension . . . subtilty and moonshine" (*Ibid.*, 356). But he pleaded on behalf of the honesty and pure fervor of these lovers of "Beauty," these believers "in miracle . . . in inspiration, and in ecstasy" (*Ibid.*, 335).

Here Emerson certainly seems to have been painting his own portrait, since he would describe himself to Lidian two months later as "a poet . . . a rainbow or a firefly." He insisted in a letter to his Aunt Mary, however, that in the lecture he had been "describing a class of young persons whom I have seen—I hope it is not confession and that, past all hope, I am confounded with my compassionated heroes & heroines." [3] Yet Emerson *was* so "confounded," and the fault was at least partially his own. What seems clear enough, from the curious mixture of knowledgeable self-description and conscious detachment in the lecture, is that Emerson was reluctant to impale his own firefly to the lyceum boards on an inescapable pin of publicly recorded self-definition. He seems to have been careful to reserve for himself the possibility of wriggling free—a possibility that would prove useful in the 1850's, when he and Thoreau finally ceased to see eye to eye.

In fact, Emerson's insistence in the lecture that there existed "no pure Transcendentalist" (C, I, 340), and that therefore no final definition was possible, suggests how fatally easy it could be for the unwary to lump two such individualists as Emerson and Thoreau under the catch-all title *Transcendentalists,* thereby obscuring the profound differences always lurking in the term.[4] Indeed, the one thing Emerson himself insisted on in his lecture was that the Transcendentalist was essentially an idealist as opposed to the materialist—a Kantian "intuitionist" as opposed to the Lockean "sensationalist." But Thoreau, in the journal entry quoted above, would affirm that, as a Transcendentalist, he was both an idealist *and* a materialist. It was just this sort of mixture that would perplex Emerson about Whitman—a poet who was, as Ralph Rusk suggests, "in some respects, a Transcendentalist" but "one who had turned half realist and was the poet of both body and soul." [5]

Lack of agreement on definitions of Transcendentalism has a history as old as the subject itself. It characterizes some of the earliest treatments of Transcendentalism by American critics, which are still a useful starting point for the modern student.

O. B. Frothingham, for instance, in his *Transcendentalism in New England* (1876), labels William Ellery Channing a "typical Unitarian" and rejects Channing's claim to admission in the new fraternity for the following reason:

> [Channing] was certainly not a Transcendentalist in philosophy. His biographer, himself a brilliant Transcendentalist, admits as much. "His soul," he says, "was illuminated with the idea of the absolute immutable glory of the Moral Good; and reverence for conscience is the key to his whole doctrine of human destiny and duty." [6]

It is precisely on this basis that H. C. Goddard, in his *Studies in New England Transcendentalism* (1908), accepts Channing as a Transcendentalist. But, and this is of great importance for us, if "the idea of the absolute immutable glory of the Moral Good" and "reverence for conscience" constitute the heart of Channing's doctrine, they are also the secret of the Emersonian philosophy.[7] On the latter, Frothingham is fairly wide of the mark:

> Emerson does not claim for the soul a special faculty, like faith or intuition, by which truths of the spiritual order are perceived, as objects are perceived by the senses. He contends for no doctrines, whether of God or the hereafter, or the moral law, on the credit of such interior revelation.[8]

This is demonstrably untrue, and Frothingham here denies to Emerson the one tenet that finally forms the very core of Emerson's belief.

The point is worth establishing, because Goddard's valuable attempt to define Transcendentalism really turns on an implied distinction, involving this notion, between Emerson and his followers, on the one hand, and Thoreau, on the other. Frothingham had all but left Thoreau out of his study. Goddard too excludes Thoreau, but he attempts to justify his exclusion by insisting that Thoreau was "hardly more than a boy" when Transcendentalism was in its formative stage.[9] Goddard's instinct is certainly correct—Thoreau would spoil his thesis—even though his reasoning is unconvincing. Thoreau, who was born in 1817, can hardly be spoken of as being "much younger" than Margaret Fuller and Theodore Parker, both of whom were born in 1810 and are included in Goddard's study. But, more importantly, when Emerson published *Nature* in 1836, Transcendentalism was surely in its formative stage, and Thoreau was nineteen—not really "a boy," in view of the fact that he began journalizing seriously the next year.

The real crux in Goddard's book appears as his definition of Transcendentalism begins to emerge. In chronicling Bronson Alcott's conversion to the new thought, Goddard quotes the following from Alcott's diary:

> [After reading Coleridge] I was led deeper to seek the grounds even of experience, and found the elements of human consciousness not in the impressions of external nature, but in the spontaneous life of Spirit itself, independent of experience in space and time. Thus was I relieved from the philosophy of sense.[10]

Transcendentalism, it seems, saved Alcott from the "philosophy of sense" by removing him from the world. What is really implied, however, after we have discounted Alcott's characteristic hyperbole, is a total lack of interest in natural experience. Now this contrasts strikingly with a statement of Goddard's apropos of Emerson's interest in science: "This enthusiasm followed almost inevitably from his transcendental belief, for transcendentalism is itself a naturalistic interpretation of the world, is founded . . . on the conception of law." [11] What reconciles these two apparently contradictory statements about the nature of Transcendentalism is that the law upon which Emersonian Transcendentalism is built—the moral law—is manifestly grounded not on a naturalistic experience of the world, but much more nearly on positive ethical decrees "intuited" independently of experience. At the heart of Emersonian Transcendentalism lie neither science nor ineffable mystic ecstasy but timeless moral imperatives. Alcott's trances, we may note, brought him not joy but a homiletic trope: "He saw the entire world as one vast spinal column." [12]

Goddard makes this ethical bias clear toward the end of his book:

> [The Transcendentalists] were not proverbial metaphysicians, content in isolation from real life to spin the theory for the theory's sake; nor mystics, content to inhabit a purely subjective realm of ecstacy, oblivious to the world. They were not even primarily teachers. They were preachers. . . . Transcendentalism was a gospel. [13]

By ruling out mysticism, by calling Transcendentalism a gospel and the Transcendentalists preachers, Goddard has indirectly justified his original exclusion of Thoreau. Transcendentalism *was* a gospel—that of the moral law. Emerson, Channing, Parker, and Ripley, among others, all preached it. Thoreau, however, claimed always that he was particularly averse to moralistic preaching. Despite the fact that Goddard admits as much, and even says that Thoreau *was* a mystic, he nevertheless insists that Thoreau was "a true Transcendentalist." [14] Although there is no explanation of this contradiction, the reader of Goddard's study gradually realizes that there are two distinct kinds of Transcendentalism and Transcendentalists: the gospel preachers, Emerson *et al.*, on the one hand; and the nature mystic, Thoreau, on the other—more or less alone. [15]

In his seminal book *The Great Chain of Being*, Arthur Lovejoy makes some observations, under the heading of "The Chain of Being in Eighteenth-Century Thought, and Man's Place and Role in Nature," which are enormously illuminating for the student of American Transcendentalism. Using Professor Lovejoy's formulations as an aid, it is worth noting that many of Emerson's major ideas bear a striking resemblance to those of the Age of Reason—that Emerson, as opposed to Thoreau, is intellectually much more a man of the eighteenth century than he is of the nineteenth—and that what Orestes Brownson called "the material, soulless philosophy of the last century" [16] accounted in general for a good deal of the Transcendental gospel.

In the first place, man's position in the Great Chain, somewhere between angel and animal, endows him with a certain tragic stature—Emerson's "golden impossibility" (C, III, 66). But man's awareness of his position, both of the infinite gradations above him and of his dramatic difference from the creatures beneath him, suggests the possibility of his ascending the scale. Hence we have a justification for a belief in meliorism. This is also implied in what Lovejoy calls the "temporalizing of the Chain of Being": "The *plenum formarum* came to be conceived by some, not as the inventory but as the program of nature, which is being carried out gradually and exceedingly slowly in the cosmic history." [17] The idea that the program of nature is slowly working itself out leads to the notion that truth is "becoming" and not an eternally fixed quantity; [18] truth is identified with the *Strebung nach dem Unendlichen*. But we must notice that for Emerson (as distinct from, say, Browning) this "becoming" truth is teleological and not ethical. It has to do with the destiny of the race and not with the sanctions of personal conduct, so that it leads to the gospel of work and progress, not to any declaration of absolute moral freedom. For the eighteenth-century divines from whom Emerson got his doctrine of the immutable moral law, dogmatism in ethics was not incompatible with a belief in the necessity of political and social progress, as is demonstrated by Dr. Richard Price, Emerson's chief ethical teacher and a notorious supporter of the French Revolution.

It is interesting to note also that the belief in meliorism (the basis for eighteenth-century optimism) which we find in Emerson—"It was for good, it is to good, that all works" (C, X, 91)—also implies and contains the Emersonian principle of "Compensation." [19] As Emerson writes in the essay of that name: "For every thing you have missed, you have gained something else; and for every thing you gain, you lose something" (C, II, 98). Presumably, the thing we lose will again be replaced, that new thing lost, and so on. Is Emerson's "Compensation," then, a simple statement of universal balance, without a suggestion, finally, whether the scales tip toward good or ill? Hardly, for Emerson's drift is clearly that evil is good in disguise, and the essay ends with the clear assertion that "the compensations of calamity are made apparent to the understanding . . . after long intervals of time" (Ibid., 126). We find exactly the same progression in the Essay on Man, since Pope first tells us that

> Fortune her gifts may variously dispose,
> And these be happy call'd, unhappy those;
> But Heav'n's just balance equal will appear,
> While those are plac'd in Hope, and these in Fear:
> Not present good or ill, the joy or curse,
> But future views of better, or of worse.

Yet all, finally, is for the best:

> God sends not ill; if rightly understood,
> [For] partial ill is universal Good . . .

Perhaps the most important idea that Emerson got from the eighteenth century is the notion of Correspondence: that nature is symbolic of spiritual truth, and that to be so is, in fact, its highest and truest function. Of course, as Lovejoy points out, this idea was really inherent in the medieval formulation of the notion of the Great Chain, since the latter enabled otherworldly Christians, who scorned nature in and for itself, to accept it in the guise of an instrument: "Man might legitimately permit his mind to busy itself with the creatures and to find joy in them, so long as he used each of them as a means of passage to what lay above it on the vast slope of being."[20] Emerson, as we know, borrowed his doctrine of Correspondence from the eighteenth-century mystic Swedenborg. But Swedenborg's ideas fell on a mind which, already fertilized by the Puritan tradition and a youthful reading of Berkeley, was predisposed to view nature homiletically.[21] Furthermore, Berkeley, as Santayana has remarked, only used his idealism "argumentatively" to combat scientific materialism, not to dissolve the comfortable world in which he lived; he was no mystic.[22] For him the laws of nature were simply the laws of God. In this respect, Berkeley set the tone for an age which, with Pope, looked "thro' Nature, up to Nature's God." Thus when Emerson writes (in *English Traits*) that "science is false by not being poetic. It isolates the reptile or mollusk it assumes to explain; whilst reptile or mollusk only exists in system, in relation. The poet only sees it as an inevitable step in the path of the Creator" (C, V, 253), we realize that Emersonian Correspondence is closer to eighteenth-century Christian evolutionary theory than to anything else. Emerson's idealism was not meant to reduce the world to a solipsistic nightmare or a skeptical chaos. It was simply a way of accounting for nature "by other principles than those of carpentry and chemistry" (C, I, 63), employed by a man whose instincts were pious and not critical.

Nature, then, served Emerson as a handbook of traditional moral truth, in this respect resembling closely the "generalized" nature of the earlier eighteenth century: it was a background for human life rather than the foreground of personal experience. Art has much the same function: it is a public instrument of instruction, and the artist is therefore a public man, involved in the activity of society and pledged to be the voice of his age. On both of these vital points, which I shall explore in the following pages, Thoreau and his supposed master were essentially in conflict. Determined to keep ethics separated from ecstasy in his experience of nature and practice of art, Thoreau was indeed one of those young "collectors of the heavenly spark, with power to convey the electricity to others" (C, I, 358) whom Emerson had described in "The Transcendentalist." And more than a few sparks flew between them when Thoreau began in earnest to discharge his own lightning.

CHAPTER TWO

Emerson:

The Artist of the Prudential

I

IN 1834, Nathaniel Hawthorne published the first version of a personal allegory which was to haunt him all his life and which, as symbolic biography, was apparently far more important to him than the real story of his life. "Passages from a Relinquished Work" tells of a young man, an orphan, who is placed in the family of a certain Parson Thumpcushion, an old-line Puritan preacher. The parson's three sons, who have prospered in their environment, have become, respectively, a preacher, a physician, and a partner in a shoe store (representative, presumably, of the three estates).[1] But the orphan is different. By temperament a spectator and an artist, he vows to keep "aloof from the regular business of life," but he is fully aware of the difficulties inherent in his choice:

> This would have been a dangerous resolution anywhere in the world; it was fatal in New England. There is a grossness in the conceptions of my countrymen; they will not be convinced that any good thing may consist with what they call idleness; they can anticipate nothing but evil of a young man who neither studies physic, law, nor gospel, nor opens a store, nor takes to farming, but manifests an incomprehensible disposition to be satisfied with what his father left him.[2]

"What his father left him" is simply the desire to observe and enjoy life without the onus of a "calling"—the prototypal attribute of the artist. But, being a New Englander, the young man knows he will have to suffer isolation from his fellows and the tortures of a bad conscience. Nor will rapport with his audience assuage his solitude, for when the young man, now a travelling storyteller, goes to a distant town and performs (he tells "Mr. Higginbotham's Catastrophe"), he finds that "fame is humbug." [3] The audience responds for all the wrong reasons, and he caters to them shamelessly. What is implied, clearly, is that the artist, in attempting to reach his public, is corrupted; or perhaps the corruption is simply an objectification of the sense of guilt which the young man feels at having disobeyed Parson Thumpcushion. Indeed, in the form of his fellow traveller, Eliakim Abbott, a peregrinating preacher, the young man has his conscience palpably by his side to remind him of his transgression. So that at the end, when the orphan-artist has burnt unopened a monitory letter from Thumpcushion and made an "irrevocable choice between good and evil fate," he reports that "Eliakim groaned in spirit, and labored with tears to convince me of the guilt and madness of my life." [4]

The sop which Hawthorne has the narrator of the tale throw to his conscience is that of saying that he writes "the book for the sake of its moral, which many a dreaming youth may profit by, though it is the experience of a wandering story-teller." [5] And, indeed, Hawthorne's justification for his tales is always the useful moral that may be drawn, whatever else about them may interest the modern critic. But the one "dreaming youth" who did not profit from this moral fable was certainly Hawthorne himself. Despite the isolation, the sense of guilt, and the anguish of never feeling that he had created the thing which would justify his existence, Hawthorne remained a writer, convinced that though his choice was fatal, it was not wrong. Art was not equivalent to idleness.

But he continued to be haunted by his allegory. In "Fragments from the Journal of a Solitary Man" (1837), Hawthorne has his narrator witness the last moments of his friend Oberon, another orphan-artist solitary. In this sketch, the theme of solitude is expanded interestingly. Before offering the reader some fragments of Oberon's journal, the narrator remarks of him that "life never called the dreamer forth; it was Death that whispered him." [6] The suggestion here is that the necessary solitude of the artist—the life of contemplation and imagination—is a kind of death-in-life. Life is process, and the imagination, in attempting to fix experience, produces a stasis. This point is made clear in Hawthorne's "The Haunted Mind": it is always two o'clock in the morning when the soul of the artist begins to function, when "the imagination is a mirror." [7] This is the moment of stasis:

> Yesterday has already vanished among the shadows of the past; tomorrow has not yet emerged from the future. You have found an intermediate space, where the business of life does not intrude; where the passing moment lingers, and becomes truly the present; a spot where Father Time, when he thinks nobody is watching him, sits down by the wayside to take breath. O, that he would fall asleep, and let mortals live on without growing older! [8]

But the moment when time falls asleep is also the moment of death, as Hawthorne goes on to remind us. [9]

What should be noted here is the equating of the imaginative life with perpetual youth. The death-in-life of the artist is the need, and therefore the wish, to preserve his youthful point of view. So, to return to Oberon, we find that thankless youth, in his journal, defining his real problem: ". . . in every aspect, I loved the world so long as I could behold it with young eyes and dance through it with a young heart. The earth had been made so beautiful, that I longed for no brighter sphere, but

only an ever-youthful eternity in this." [10] Oberon's wish is
impossible, and he is therefore doomed (it seems really the
fulfillment of a deeper wish) to die at the age of twenty-five,
Hawthorne not having been willing, presumably, to allow
Oberon's solitude to give birth, in a tortured old age, to the
absurd lust which drives Thomas Mann's Aschenbach in
search of his lost youth. But the problem has at least been
clarified for us: the artist's solitude, involving not only isolation
but also his attempt to preserve and fix a vital relation to
experience, renders him pitiful and a trifle perverse.

Characteristically, Hawthorne has his narrator end the
sketch with a "beautiful moral" by quoting a section of
Oberon's journal in which the young artist describes his return
to his native village. In a penitential and benevolent mood, he
decides to admonish any would-be youthful emulator of his
"wild life and worthless fame":

> 'He shall be taught,' said I, 'by my life, and by my death, that
> the world is a sad one for him who shrinks from its sober
> duties. My experience shall warn him to adopt some great and
> serious aim, such as manhood will cling to, that he may not
> feel himself, too late, a cumberer of this overladen earth, but a
> man among men. I will beseech him not to follow an eccentric
> path, nor, by stepping aside from the highway of human
> affairs, to relinquish his claim upon human sympathy. And
> often, as a text of deep and varied meaning, I will remind him
> that he is an American.' [11]

Hawthorne's retraction does not ring true. The letter from
Parson Thumpcushion has been destroyed, and there is no
going home. But considering how strong is the fantasy of
reconciliation, one marvels at Hawthorne's artistic resolve.
Such guilt feelings might have undermined a less committed
writer, as, indeed, they seem finally to have done to Emerson.
But not even the American fervor (if such it was) that

produced "The Life of Franklin Pierce" could prevent Hawthorne from writing *The Marble Faun,* a book which Emerson
considered "mere mush." [12]

II

After reading Hawthorne's "Footprints on the Sea-Shore"
in 1838, Emerson complained to Elizabeth Peabody "that there
was no inside to it. Alcott and he together would make a man"
(*J*, IV, 479). Admittedly, the sketch is slight and somewhat
precious; but that Emerson would fail, for all the blandness of
treatment, to be caught up by Hawthorne's theme is a little
curious. Thematically, "Footprints" has more inside to it than
Nature. In it Hawthorne returns once again to his pet subject,
solitude. The narrator, a solitary man, begs to be allowed, at
least for a day, to become a "peaceful outlaw," to retire into his
private world of "fantasies and recollections, or anticipated
realities." [13] The major purpose of the day's ramble, as reflected
in the title of the sketch, is presumably the narrator's attempt to
retrace his steps, to fix himself in a moment of time and track
his "own nature in its wayward course." [14] The successive
stages of this experiment in stasis are paralleled, in the sketch,
by the solitary's encounters with a group of three lively young
girls, who will finally save him from the oppressiveness of his
dangerous voyage back into time.

At the first stage of the descent, simple reflection, the
narrator has literally his own tracks to follow, and they guide
him "with an observing consciousness through every unconscious wandering of thought and fancy." [15] He does not yet
seriously need human contact and therefore only sees the girls
at a great distance. But when the solitary begins to peer deeply
into the pool of past being, the girls are closer at hand and, in
fact, disturb his visions (pleasantly, he admits) by bathing
their feet in the pool. Soon after, when the solitary begins to
rave out loud, he is checked by the realization that the girls are

observing him. Finally, at the close of day, when the place has
become dismal and the narrator feels haunted by gloomy
fantasies, his melancholy is relieved by his first real meeting
with the youngsters as they call out to invite him to dinner.
From the death-in-life which is the necessary condition of his
imagination, the artist is saved, at least temporarily, by real
contact with the world, particularly the world of youth.

Perhaps it is not, after all, surprising that Emerson saw
nothing in "Footprints on the Sea-Shore" (which is certainly
one of Hawthorne's minor sketches), considering that a few
years later he was to insist that Hawthorne's writing was not
good for anything. But Emerson's obtuseness when faced with
Hawthorne's obsessive theme is still curious, since Emerson
was obviously neither unaware of nor unconcerned with the
problem himself. Emerson's journal entry after Hawthorne's
funeral makes this clear: "I thought there was a tragic element
in the event, that might be more fully rendered,—in the
painful solitude of the man, which, I suppose, could no longer
be endured, and he died of it" (J, X, 39–40). Emerson's "I
suppose" is what gives us pause here. Did he himself not know
how painful solitude might be? Or does his distant tone mask a
vague disapproval of Hawthorne's way of life—his over-
intense concern for the dangers and pleasures of the imagination?

It is clear enough that Emerson needed society for well-
being. He complained of loneliness when Lidian and his
mother went off on holidays and left him to himself, and he
could note quite honestly in his journal: "Now and then a man
exquisitely made can and must live alone; but coop up most
men, and you undo them" (J, VIII, 462). Yet Emerson was
always to insist on the necessity of solitude, particularly for the
scholar: "He must embrace solitude as a bride . . . go cherish
your soul; expel companions; set your habits to a life of
solitude" (C, I, 173–74). In this passage (from "Literary

Ethics" [1838]), Emerson's advice seems particularly stringent: "Do not go into solitude only that you may presently come into public. Such solitude denies itself; is public and stale" (*Ibid.*, 174). But there follows a characteristic equivocation: "Of course I would not have any superstition about solitude. Let the youth study the uses of solitude and of society. Let him use both, not serve either" (*Ibid.*, 175). This point of view is offered most notably in "Self-Reliance":

> It is easy in the world to live after the world's opinion; it is easy in solitude to live after our own; but the great man is he who in the midst of the crowd keeps with perfect sweetness the independence of solitude. (*C*, II, 53–54)

For Emerson the *via media* was apparently a viable solution. But Hawthorne had found that, however much the artist may crave society, the world corrupts: Owen Warland's pitiful attempts to compromise (in "The Artist of the Beautiful") always led to the destruction of his dream. Emerson, to be sure, could write in "The Over-Soul": "Men descend to meet" (*C*, II, 278). But meet, finally, they must.

It is clear that for Emerson the possibility of corruption was greater in solitude than in society. In his journal entry for March 2, 1822, the young Emerson debated the question with himself:

> . . . what are the springs of action, which incite any one man to do noble and praiseworthy deeds?—Patriotism, Love, Emulation. And where were these begotten?—in Heaven? in unreal and fictitious scenes? in the silent groves, and the solitary hut of the ascetic? No; these form the atmosphere and the bond of union to *social*, cultivated, and active Man. Solitude has but few sacrifices to make, and may be innocent, but can hardly be greatly virtuous. . . . Great actions, from their nature, are not done in a closet; they are performed in the face of the sun, and in behalf of the world. (*Jn*, I, 98)

To be sure, Emerson does not yet positively equate solitude with evil. But he does certainly connect virtue with public action, adumbrating even here the burden of his theories about the proper end of art. Indeed, will art be allowed at all? That which is done in a closet seems somehow suspect. Moreover, solitude may have appeared innocent to Emerson on March 2nd, but on the next day he thought better of the matter: "Is solitude purer than Society? Eve yielded in solitude to the tempter, and the sin was done in retired shades, which 'brought death into the world, and all our woe' " (*Ibid.*, 99).

These sentiments are not simply samples of Emerson's boyish priggishness. In 1834, twelve years after meditating on Eve, Emerson reiterated his conclusion in another journal remark: "Is not the use of society to educate the Will, which never would acquire force in solitude? We mean will, when we say that a person has a good deal of character." Shortly thereafter he added: "Luther and Napoleon are better treatises on the Will than Edwards's" (*J*, III, 249–50). Edwards, of course, identified the benevolent will with the affections of the heart—a perception of God's excellency and a leaning towards it. Since the will to good is dependent on grace, solitude is, in Edwards' view, no more dangerous than society. But for Emerson man alone with himself was somehow not to be trusted, and the world's work was preferable to private dreams.

Emerson really leaned toward this opinion in "Literary Ethics" (although, as we have already noted, he seemed to be straddling the fence on the question of solitude). He warned the would-be man of letters against isolation: "Extricating themselves from the tasks of the world, the world revenges itself by exposing, at every turn, the folly of these incomplete, pedantic, useless, ghostly creatures . . . [the scholar] must bear his share of the common load. He must work with men in houses, and not with their names in books." Emerson offered Napoleon as the man to be emulated—"Means to ends, is the motto of all his behavior"—and approved of the gospel of activity: "Feudalism and Orientalism had long enough thought it majestic to do nothing; the modern majesty consists in work" (*C*, I, 177–79). Yet when Orestes Brownson considered this Dartmouth address in *The Boston Quarterly Review*, he let Emerson's equivocal advice carry him in the wrong direction. The burden of Emerson's talk had certainly been that scholarship and art are ultimately the means to an end and that solitude is dangerous. Brownson took him to task for saying the opposite:

> We find also some difficulty in admitting the notion that the scholar must be a solitary soul, living apart and in himself alone; that he must shun the multitude and mingle never in the crowd, or if he mingle, never as one of the crowd; that to him the thronged mart and the peopled city must be a solitude; that he must commune only with his own thoughts, and study only the mysteries of his own being. We have no faith in this ascetic discipline. Its tendency is to concentrate the scholar entirely within himself, to make him a mere individual, without connexions or sympathies with his race; and to make him utter his own individual life, not the life of the nation, much less the universal life of Humanity. . . . The scholar must have an end to which his scholarship serves as a means.[16]

Brownson scorned what he took to be Emerson's advice to the scholar: "He must be an artist, his sole end is to produce a work of art. He must scorn to create for a purpose, to compel his genius to serve, to work for an end beyond the work itself." If Emerson had said this, Brownson thought him mistaken; but was this Emerson's view? To a reader with hindsight, Brownson's concluding remarks, though not appropriate to Emerson, seem strikingly prophetic of another, more dangerous man to come. The true American writer, said Brownson, will not win that title merely "because he has lived apart, refused to 'serve

society,' held lone reveries, and looked on sunsets, and sunrise." [17] How would Brownson cope with Henry Thoreau?
Even Emerson was to find that difficult.

Emerson probably read Brownson's review. At any rate,
Emerson's 1839 lecture on "Demonology" contained a clear
rebuke to any young men who might have been contemplating
a retreat to a dark world of their own. He declared his
disapproval of the idea that "fortunate men, fortunate youths
exist, whose good is not virtue or the public good, but a private
good, robbed from the rest. It is a midsummer-madness, corrupting all who hold the tenet" (C, X, 19–20). More
significantly, perhaps, Emerson entered this remark in his
journal for 1841: "Every sensual pleasure is private and mortal: every spiritual action is public and generative" (J, VI, 6).
Considering what we have noted about Emerson's view of
solitude, it would seem fair to construe his remark another
way: every private pleasure is sensual, and every public action
is spiritual. The dark world of art seems to imply secret and
illicit pleasure—the onanism of the soul. Hawthorne, as we
have seen, was fully and painfully aware of the necessary
connection between artistic creation and death. So, too, was
Emerson. In "Art" (1841) he finally got around to warning
against these dangers in a way which must have at least
partially soothed Brownson:

> They [artists] abhor men as tasteless, dull, and inconvertible,
> and console themselves with color-bags and blocks of marble.
> They reject life as prosaic, and create a death which they call
> poetic. They despatch the day's weary chores, and fly to
> voluptuous reveries. They eat and drink, that they may
> afterwards execute the ideal. Thus is art vilified . . . and
> struck with death from the first. (C, II, 367)

Although Emerson's major purpose here is clearly to offer his
theory of "natural art," drawn from and relating to common

life, this passage is also an implied attack on the school of *ars gratia artis,* which we have come to associate with the name of Poe. Emerson is squarely against the artist's having a private ideal: "As soon as beauty is sought . . . for pleasure, it degrades the seeker" (C, II, 366). The way in which beauty must be useful, the ideal which Emerson would finally have the artist serve, is made clear in another passage from "Art":

> Art has not yet come to its maturity if it do not put itself abreast with the most potent influences of the world, if it is not practical and moral, if it do not stand in connection with the conscience, if it do not make the poor and uncultivated feel that it addresses them with a voice of lofty cheer. There is higher work for Art than the arts. They are abortive births of an imperfect or vitiated instinct. (C, II, 363)

The perfect society will have no need of art. Meanwhile, the artist has a responsibility to instruct and enliven, and his art should be a vehicle for duty. Hawthorne's Artist of the Beautiful is effeminate and self-indulgent, and his art is so much death.

The real source for Emerson's view on the end of art is, of course, eighteenth-century neoclassical aesthetic theory; and this influence, though an early one, was never really discarded by the mature Emerson. In early journal entries Emerson's debt is apparent, both in style and in thought:

> We require such works as the Rambler & books of that description, moral & learned & argumentative writers, minds of a firmer make, built up to persuade & convince the stubborn, employing themselves in encountering prejudices & detecting frauds, in checking & chastising profane abuse, & subjecting to controul those . . . passions which corrode & fret the soul.
>
> Such works are rare in our american literature & we all feel the deficiency & the want of them is the reproach under which we have long impatiently laboured. Books of an ephemeral

nature like the sketchbook will not remedy the evil. Although we feel the beauty of his description, although we love the picturesque glitter of a summer morning's landscape as much as any yet we would willingly exchange the transient pleasure for . . . those of active & salutary effect whose tendency is to instruct & improve rather than to entertain. (*Jn*, I, 172)

This is Emerson in 1820, and his attitude on the value of contemplating the sunrise remarkably resembles that of Orestes Brownson in his attack on Emerson nineteen years later. What is especially interesting here, moreover, is that Emerson's version of the eighteenth-century dictum on the purpose of art—"to instruct & improve rather than to entertain"—strongly stresses the didactic. Dr. Johnson (whose *Prefaces* Emerson read early) set the tone for his age, echoing Horace, by avowing that the purpose of poetry is "to instruct by pleasing." But the young Emerson apparently was willing to do without the entertainment in favor of solid instruction.

Although the great Cham of literature had seen fit, for example, to overlook moral lapses in Shakespeare's plays in view of his great artistic power, the young Emerson found much of Shakespeare unrelievedly disgusting and impure, and corrupting in its influence. He preferred "the authors of the Tatler, Spectator, Rambler, & Adventurer" because they "censured vice with wit and recommended virtuous principles in moral strains so artfully that they could not displease" (*Jn*, I, 331). And in 1824, Emerson could praise Alexander Pope for much the same reason: "Mr. Pope's judicious poems, the Moral Essays and Essay on Man . . . without originality, seize upon all the popular speculations floating among sensible men and give them in a compact graceful form to the following age" (*J*, I, 392). Nor did his attitude change much later on. To be sure, in *English Traits* (1856), while in a mood of general disaffection with the English eighteenth century, Emerson dismissed Pope cavalierly as the man who "wrote poetry fit to put round frosted cake" (C, V, 255). But in his journal for the same year he called Pope "the best and only readable English poet" (J, VIII, 98).

What Emerson's basic position was can be seen, from another direction, by a consideration of some of his comments on Wordsworth. In 1826 he accused Wordsworth of failing to please "by being too much a poet" (J, II, 106), meaning clearly that by violating the Johnsonian canon of "general nature," Wordsworth had allowed his instruction to get lost in a welter of detail. The praise of Wordsworth which followed was based entirely on the "Ode: Intimations of Immortality . . .": "He has nobly embodied a sentiment, which, I know not why, has always seemed congenial to humanity, that the soul has come to us from a pre-existence in God" (J, II, 109). Still, not even the noble sentiments of the "Ode," nor the exciting new thought which Emerson had headily imbibed from Coleridge's *Aids to Reflection* in 1829, were sufficient to prevent him from condemning Wordsworth and Coleridge, on his return from Europe in 1833, for being "deficient,—in insight into religious truth. They have no idea of that species of moral truth which I call the first philosophy." [18] For Emerson, Art had a higher work than mere poetry, and nature ecstasy smacked suspiciously of moral turpitude. When he reconsidered Wordsworth in *English Traits*, it was again the "Ode" he singled out, calling it the intellectual "high-water mark" of the age (C, V, 298). There, at least, Emerson found some moral sentiments that might serve all men as a guide and support.

In his position, then, as literary critic, Emerson's attitude was frequently much that of a preacher who will admit an occasional rhetorical trope or flourish in order to hold his congregation and prevent their falling asleep, so long as the doctrine is not swallowed up in the fable. If Richard Mather's warning in the *Bay Psalm Book* that "God's Altar needs not our pollishings" was unfamiliar to Emerson, he at least had the words of his doggedly orthodox Aunt Mary in his journal, quoted approvingly in 1824:

> As to words or languages being so important—I'll have nothing of it. The images, the sweet immortal images are within us—born there, our native right, and sometimes one kind of sounding word or syllable awakens the instrument of our souls, and sometimes another. But we are not slaves to sense any more than to political usurpers, but by fashion and imbecility. Aye, if I understand you, so you think. (J, I, 334)

So, apparently, did Emerson think throughout his life. In 1838 he adorned his journal with the following statement of moral purpose: "Literature is an amusement; virtue is the business of the universe" (J, V, 102). The sentiment was repeated, less stridently, in 1847: "I think the whole use in literature is the moral" (J, VII, 250). But perhaps the real spirit behind Emerson's attitude is most clearly visible in a journal entry of 1844: "Pure intellect is the pure devil when you have got off all the masks of Mephistopheles. It is a painful symbol to me that the index or forefinger is always the most soiled of all the fingers" (J, VI, 497). We are carried back to the attitudes of the American seventeenth century, and one is reminded of that spare but powerful admonition of the Puritans that *"Jesus Christ* is not got with a wet finger." [19] Art, truly, seems a creation of the devil.

The artist, of course, may secretly share this view. But what is he to do if the art which the world demands—an art that, in Emerson's words, "builds, adds and affirms" (C, VIII, 37)—revolts his soul? If, with Thomas Mann's Adrian Leverkühn, he keeps his painful pact with the devil not out of sheer perversity, but simply because "with his whole soul he despises the positivism of the world for which one would save him, the lie of its godliness," what is there to do but "sign-off" from an active, bustling nineteenth-century America? The decision is difficult: Adrian Leverkühn's "No!" uttered "to false and flabby middle-class piety" is described by Mann as "proudly despairing." [20] Even when the artist is secure in the value of his offering, he must still bear the burden of guilt and shame at being called idle and perhaps evil.

So, too, Hawthorne: his artistic alter ego, Oberon (in "The Devil in Manuscript"), is in a state of despair at having devoted his life to lurid dreams and phantasms. Still, he knows that in his writings is the recollection of the night when he walked "along a hilly road, on a starlight October evening; in the pure and bracing air, I became all soul, and felt as if I could climb the sky, and run a race along the Milky Way." [21] But will the pride of such a memory outweigh the guilt of feeling that a devil is also in his manuscripts? Oberon's friend, the pious and acquiescing side of Hawthorne, fears the writings and is really in favor of their being destroyed. But something else gives him pause: ". . . all at once, I remembered passages of high imagination, deep pathos, original thoughts, and points of such varied excellence, that the vastness of the sacrifice struck me most forcibly." [22] Yet guilt wins out, and Oberon throws the manuscripts into the fire, whereupon the devil is released, and the house and town catch fire. What are we finally to believe? The greater evil, it would seem, lies in the destruction of Oberon's works, not in their preservation. Perhaps the devil is in activity and not in the hermetic contemplations of the artist. Maybe the true villain of the story is Hawthorne's timorous narrator, who has not enough faith in art to prevent the destruction of Oberon's creations

Thoreau, like Hawthorne's Oberon, was also guilty of setting the world on fire; and, at least according to himself, the fault was really the world's and not his own. If, as Perry Miller suggests,[23] Thoreau's relation of the story is an attempt at guilty self-justification, we can perhaps guess at what was

bothering him. What shamed Thoreau was not the fire, but the
fact that on the day he set the Concord woods ablaze, he was
"no better employed than [his] townsmen" (*W*, VIII, 25). His
shameful descent into the world's work may not have
amounted to any more than a bit of "trivial fishing" (*Ibid.*, 23),
but it still kept him from his true business of attending to
nature's phenomena. If we take the story as a parable, spawned
by the failure of *A Week on the Concord and Merrimack
Rivers*, perhaps Thoreau was really trying to say that he was
less of a rascal as a contemplative writer than he was as an
active Concordian: the devil in manuscript was hardly as
dangerous as the devil out of it.

Emerson, who played the role of Hawthornian narrator to
Thoreau's Oberon, was apparently not a great deal of help to
his young protégé. The older man may have believed that "the
one prudence in life is concentration; the one evil is dissipa-
tion" (*C*, VI, 73); but how was one to concentrate while
straddling two worlds? If solitary contemplation was evil and
idleness, and society trivial, the way certainly was not clear.
What was clear to Thoreau, as he confided to his journal in
1837, was that contemplation had to precede action: "My
desire is to know *what* I have lived, that I may know *how* to
live henceforth" (*W*, VII, 9). If it turned out that life was to
be spent in exploring privately the *what* of existence, so much
the worse for the world.

III

It is a peculiarity (I find by observation upon others) of
humour in me, my strong propensity for strolling. I deliberately shut up my books in a cloudy July noon, put on my old
clothes and old hat and slink away to the whortleberry bushes
and slip with the greatest satisfaction into a little cowpath
where I am sure I can defy observation. This point gained, I
solace myself for hours with picking blueberries and other

trash of the woods, far from fame, behind the birch-trees. I
seldom enjoy hours as I do these. I remember them in winter; I
expect them in spring. (*J*, II, 244–45)

Even a reader only passingly familiar with Thoreau's writings
would probably not hesitate in identifying this paragraph. The
love of solitary walking and old clothes, the transcendent joys
of huckleberrying, and the keen dependence on the revolution
of the seasons—all these point unmistakably to Thoreau. Yet
this passage was inscribed in his journal for 1828 by
Emerson—one of the very few such passages to be found in
Emerson's writings. Perhaps the passion for idle berry-picking
is a sign of adolescence. If so, Thoreau never grew up.
Emerson, at any rate, had apparently ceased to remember his
golden hours, *procul negotiis*, by 1851, when he jotted down in
his journal a notable sentence which, in enlarged form, was to
serve as part of his funeral oration on Thoreau eleven years
later: "Thoreau wants a little ambition in his mixture. Fault of
this, instead of being the head of American engineers, he is
captain of huckleberry party" (*J*, VIII, 228). Emerson wrote
this in July 1851, and quite apart from the large shift in values
on Emerson's part that it exhibits, there is clearly a personal
animus in the statement.

ANimosity

   What exactly happened to cause a blowup of the friendship between the two no one knows. But it is clear that a
breach occurred. Emerson, as one can tell from his journal, was
always and increasingly distressed by what he called Thoreau's
lack of sweetness, by his nay-saying, and especially by his
captiously paradoxical habits of expression. Emerson was to re-
express his displeasure with these latter two traits in his
biographical sketch of Thoreau. But curiously (or perhaps not
so curiously), Emerson was only belaboring Thoreau for char-
acteristics which, as he knew well enough, had helped to form
his own difficult personality. There was certainly a nay-sayer in
Emerson; in 1833 he wrote in his journal the very Thoreauvian

"I like the sayers of No better than the sayers of Yes" (*J*, III, 122). As for paradox, in his essay "Prudence" (1841) Emerson advised his readers to avoid direct "hostility and bitterness" in conversation with friends by using this harmless trick of rhetoric:

> Though your views are in straight antagonism to theirs, assume an identity of sentiment, assume that you are saying precisely that which all think, and in the flow of wit and love roll out your paradoxes in solid column, with not the infirmity of a doubt. So at least shall you get an adequate deliverance. (*C*, II, 239)

If the young Thoreau did build his style on Emerson's advice, he may indeed have found that it gave him "adequate deliverance," but unfortunately it made his older friend uncomfortable. Negativism and paradox were interesting, Emerson probably found, as part of a literary program, but they were hardly useful in constructing a cooperative American society.

As for Thoreau, he undoubtedly felt that his antagonism was good for something: "One must not complain that his friend is cold, for heat is generated between them." This justification of his ways Thoreau put in his journal on January 30, 1852, and then quickly added his own criticism of Emerson: "I doubt if Emerson could trundle a wheelbarrow through the streets, because it would be out of character. One needs to have a comprehensive character" (*W*, IX, 250). Quite clearly, Henry thought Waldo pompous. Two days later Thoreau registered his disapproval of Emerson's patronizing attitude toward him (*Ibid.*, 256). Thoreau obviously felt that Emerson's success had changed him and ruined their friendship. On December 17, 1851, Thoreau had written this spirited paragraph in his journal:

> One of the best men I know often offends me by uttering made words—the very best words, of course, or dinner

speeches, most smooth and gracious and fluent repartees, a sort
of talking to Buncombe, a dash of polite conversation, a
graceful bending, as if I were Master Slingsby of promising
parts, from the University. O would you but be simple and
downright! Would you but cease your palaver! It is the
misfortune of being a gentleman and famous. (*W*, IX, 141)

There is no doubt that Thoreau is here complaining of Emerson, the condescending mentor, who in winning a public had
somehow gone over to the other side. Moreover, it seems clear
that Thoreau was considerably distressed by what he took to be
Emerson's genteel fence-straddling—his hypocritically seeming to be one man and turning out to be another. Thoreau
went to the trouble, on December 12, 1851, of copying into his
journal a passage from one of Emerson's books, "which it
happens that I rarely look at" (he was decidedly not in a
grateful mood). Significantly, the passage is from "Literary
Ethics," which, as we have already noticed, contains some
rather ambiguous advice to aspiring young writers. What
caught Thoreau's eye was not the inconclusive discussion of
solitude, nor the section extolling activity, but rather a passage
which follows an exhortation that the artist be open and frank:

> "If, with a high trust, he can thus submit himself, he will find
> that ample returns are poured into his bosom out of what
> seemed hours of obstruction and loss. Let him not grieve too
> much on account of unfit associates. . . . In a society of
> perfect sympathy, no word, no act, no record, would be. He
> will learn that it is not much matter what he reads, what he
> does. Be a scholar, and he shall have the scholar's part of
> everything," etc., etc. (*W*, IX, 134)

Thoreau was obviously in a highly ironical mood, for his
inconsequent comment on the passage is simply that its moral
is obvious: "I had, perhaps, *thought* the same thing myself
twenty times during the day, and yet had not been *contented*

with that account of it, leaving me thus to be amused by the coincidence, rather than impressed as by an intimation out of the deeps" (*Ibid.,* 135).

What makes this especially interesting is that Thoreau himself has rendered Emerson's thought commonplace by leaving out the key sentence. The four dots after "associates" mark the omission of the following: "When he sees how much thought he owes to the disagreeable antagonism of various persons who pass and cross him, he can easily think that" (C, I, 184). Thoreau is clearly playing a game, tweaking Emerson's nose with impunity in the privacy of his journal. Thoreau had been open and frank, and his antagonism had only served to alienate Emerson. Was Emerson honest in giving advice that he himself could not swallow? Perhaps, then, Thoreau felt that Emerson deserved having the pith cut out of his paragraph. As it stands, expurgated by Thoreau's own hand, the passage is certainly not the account of the matter that *contented* Thoreau. It needs the extra sentence. But that, Thoreau reserved for himself; after all, it was he, not Emerson, who thrived on antagonism.

In all probability, Thoreau was bitter about the failure of *A Week,* particularly in the face of Emerson's manifest success. It was an angry book and in many ways a very un-Transcendental one, not at all uniformly benign and uplifting like the older man's publications. Yet Emerson had seemed to approve of the manuscript. What was the matter?

The matter, from Emerson's point of view, was simply that Henry's "crotchets" [24] were getting on his nerves, and it must have occurred to the sage of Concord that his crying up a young man with a reputation for atheism, idleness, and angularity could hardly help his own career. It is, for instance, interesting to speculate about why Emerson put off Theodore Parker's request that he review Thoreau's first book: "I am not the man to write the Notice of Thoreau's book. I am of the same clan & parish. You must give it to a good foreigner." [25] He must have known that his own praise, at this crucial phase of Thoreau's career, would carry a great deal of weight. But it seems clear that Emerson wanted to see the direction of the wind before making his own public statement. The "American claim & ensign" he wanted for the book before sending it abroad was hardly promising: Lowell's faint praise was of little use, and George Ripley's reservations because of Thoreau's anti-Christian, anti-biblical bias were bound to be damaging. When the English opinions finally came, they were not good.

Indeed, Emerson could undoubtedly foresee the dangers on June 15, 1849, just four days after he declined to review *A Week,* when Parker, responding to Emerson, noted that there was "a good deal of sauciness, & a good deal of affectation in the book," which Parker blamed on Thoreau's "trying to be R. W. Emerson." [26] It would certainly not do Emerson any good to have Thoreau's faults ascribed to him. Revolutionary tendencies might have been pleasing to Emerson in 1836; they were much less so thirteen years later. One might conjecture with safety that Emerson's awareness of the danger in Thoreau was sharpening: Thoreau represented the side of Emerson—rebellious, unsocial, brooding, and in love with artistic "idleness"—which the older man increasingly came to dislike and wished to suppress. Huckleberrying days were over by 1851.

Emerson's stricture on Thoreau in his funeral oration of 1862 sums up one of the poignant literary misunderstandings of nineteenth-century America. From Thoreau's side, it is the story of how a writer painfully dedicated to his craft—one who defined his whole purpose in life in an earnestly underlined statement to the president of Harvard explaining his reason for wanting to use the library: *"because I have chosen letters for my profession"* [27]—failed to get sympathy from the one person in his world who should have understood. From Emerson's side, the funeral oration exhibits an apparent loss of belief in the value of the artist's job:

> . . . I cannot help counting it a fault in him that he had no ambition. Wanting this, instead of engineering for all America, he was the captain of a huckleberry-party. Pounding beans is good to the end of pounding empires one of these days; but if, at the end of years, it is still only beans! (C, X, 480)

Emerson returned here to the standards of Napoleon, as expressed in "Literary Ethics": "Means to ends, is the motto of all his behavior" (C, I, 179). But Emerson knew—or should have remembered—since he had read *Walden,* that for Thoreau beans were better than empires, since they led in fact to things far more valuable than beans: "When my hoe tinkled against the stones, that music echoed to the woods and the sky, and was an accompaniment to my labor which yielded an instant and immeasurable crop. It was no longer beans that I hoed, nor I that hoed beans" (W, II, 175). At the end of years, it was not only beans, but beans plus the kind of ecstasy that served Thoreau as the basis for his art.

As for the huckleberry party, Emerson, as we have noted, had once been aware from personal experience that huckleberrying implied far more than time idly spent in picking trash; in Thoreau's words, "at the same time that we exclude mankind from gathering berries in our field, we exclude them from gathering health and happiness and inspiration and a hundred other far finer and nobler fruits than berries" (W, XX, 56). In this sense, Thoreau made huckleberries his theme all his life, as he did beans or apples or anything else in nature that yielded an experience worth recording. Pounding empires might be as good as pounding beans, he undoubtedly thought; but if, at the end of years, it is only possessions and power, how shall an author justify his existence? Words, not deeds, are his stock in trade.

But Emerson, it seems, was never entirely convinced that words were enough. To be sure, in "The Poet" he attacked that materialistic criticism "which assumes that manual skill and activity is the first merit of all men, and disparages such as say and do not, overlooking the fact that some men, namely poets, are natural sayers, sent into the world to the end of expression" (C, III, 7). Nevertheless, Emerson admitted the possibility of fakery: there are those "whose province is action but who quit it to imitate the sayers" (*Ibid.*). Perhaps it was uneasiness about this danger which then led him to justify poetry in an equivocal manner: "Words are also actions, and actions are a kind of words" (*Ibid.*, 8). Whatever else it means, the statement clearly implies that words should be actions, that poetry should function directly in the world's work.

Emerson frequently makes this point explicitly. In "Inspiration," for instance: "What is best in literature is the affirming, prophesying, spermatic words of men-making poets. Only that is poetry which cleanses and mans me" (C, VIII, 294). Or in "Prudence": "Poets should be lawgivers; that is, the boldest lyric inspiration should not chide and insult, but should announce and lead the civil code and the day's work" (C, II, 231). And in "Poetry and Imagination": "The trait and test of the poet is that he builds, adds and affirms. The critic destroys: the poet says nothing but what helps somebody" (C, VIII, 37). The writer of poetry is a poet so long as his poems are an exhortation to positive action. But when he retires to a private world of subjective experience, he is an idler, perhaps even a fraud.

Yet Emerson seemed to make a great deal out of the

necessary inactivity of the Transcendentalist. Perhaps the best
of all such statements occurs in his lecture on "The Transcendentalist," delivered in January 1842:

> New, we confess, and by no means happy, is our condition: if
> you want the aid of our labor, we ourselves stand in greater
> want of the labor. We are miserable with inaction. We perish
> of rest and rust: but we do not like your work.
>   'Then,' says the world, 'show me your own.'
>   'We have none.'
>   'What will you do, then?' cries the world.
>   'We will wait.'
>   'How long?'
>   'Until the universe beckons and calls us to work.'
>   'But whilst you wait, you grow old and useless.'
>   'Be it so: I can sit in a corner and *perish* (as you call it), but
> I will not move until I have the highest command. If no call
> should come for years, for centuries, then I know that the
> want of the Universe is the attestation of faith by my
> abstinence.' (C, I, 350–51)

Nowhere do we find a more eloquent defense of the noble
idleness of the spiritual man. Emerson has described the
prototype of Melville's anti-hero Bartleby, whose refusal to
participate in the hustling nineteenth century is an avowal of
high faith in his own humanness. And yet, if Bartleby was
meant to be the type of the artist, Emerson was apparently not
prepared to cry with Melville, "Ah, Bartleby! Ah, humanity!"
A world given over to materialism might justify Transcendental *inaction;* but Emerson by no means meant to imply thereby
that a retreat into the world of art was the solution. This is
made clear in Emerson's "Lecture on the Times," delivered one
month before "The Transcendentalist":

> The genius of the day does not incline to a deed, but to a
> beholding. It is not that men do not wish to act; they pine to
> be employed, but are paralyzed by the uncertainty what they

should do. The inadequacy of the work to the faculties is the painful perception which keeps them still. This happens to the best. Then, talents bring their usual temptations, and the current literature and poetry with perverse ingenuity draw us away from life to solitude and meditation. (*C*, I, 283)

Clearly, literature is a *pis aller,* a perverse temptation to which the gifted idle are liable.

Indeed, there is little doubt that one side of Emerson considered the artist an idler and art a luxury—"the overflowing phantasms of a high-fed animal" (*J*, I, 261). In a lecture delivered in January 1841, "Man the Reformer," he insisted that the artist do his share of the world's work. Emerson does allow that the poet may find manual labor not only not congenial to, but downright destructive of, intellectual work; but he undercuts this allowance:

> Yet I will suggest that no separation from labor can be without some loss of power and of truth to the seer himself; that, I doubt not, the faults and vices of our literature and philosophy, their too great fineness, effeminacy, and melancholy, are attributable to the enervated and sickly habits of the literary class. Better that the book should not be quite so good, and the book-maker abler and better, and not himself often a ludicrous contrast to all that he has written. (*C*, I, 242)

Hawthorne was to make a practical experiment in labor just three months later, at Brook Farm, and was to find it "the curse of the world": "nobody can meddle with it without becoming proportionably brutified!" [28] But Emerson, more innocent of such experience than Hawthorne, seems to associate literary and artistic virtues with muscular development in the service of society.

Interestingly and characteristically, however, ten days after making this public statement Emerson contradicted it privately in his journal: "If I judge from my own experience I should unsay all my fine things, I fear, concerning the manual labor of literary men. They ought to be released from every species of public or private responsibility. To them the grasshopper is a burden" (*J*, V, 517). Duplicity was his besetting sin, and he had recognized it a few years earlier: "Am I a hypocrite, who am disgusted by vanity everywhere and preach self-trust every day?" [29]

In view of these ambivalent attitudes, it is easy to see why the problem of whether or not the writer is justified in devoting his life to his craft plagued Emerson constantly. If the steady rise, after 1836, of his reputation as a public orator justified his escape from the pulpit in 1832 and dispelled the aura of disrespectability from his choice of writing as a profession, this still did not entirely ease his conscience. Indeed, it probably exacerbated his distress. The young man who had thought it sufficient to be "infinite spectator, without hurrying, uncalled, to be infinite doer," and who was determined instead to "brood on his immortality" (*J*, III, 462) soon found himself saying that "the modern majesty consists in work" (*C*, I, 179). If, on the one hand, he could now hope to win the approbation of his neighbors, was he not, on the other, selling short the young poet in himself who, willingly forgetful of house and food, wanted only to become the "fool of ideas" (*C*, I, 210)?

It is very likely that Emerson's variable attitude toward Thoreau was a measure of his own inner conflict. Thoreau, in his flamboyant intransigence, was a continual reminder to Emerson of the extent to which he had abandoned his earlier standards. Furthermore, Thoreau was clearly much more a man of action than Emerson: he could make pencils, survey property, and do all kinds of necessary jobs. To this extent, Thoreau was surely more the engineer of Concord society than Emerson and, though odd, the kind of man that his neighbors could understand. Yet Thoreau, as he confided to his journal in 1851, was fiercely determined to maintain physical and spiritual independence: "If I should sell both my forenoons and afternoons to society, neglecting my peculiar calling, there would be nothing left worth living for. I trust that I shall never thus sell my birthright for a mess of potage" (*W*, VIII, 141). By this time, having returned from his second European tour, Emerson was thoroughly involved in his professional career, devoting both fore- and afternoons to lecturing far and wide. Perhaps, then, when he took Thoreau to task for having no ambition, he was really venting his own guilty anger at Thoreau's freedom. Emerson was less his own man than his independent young friend. Indeed, it was Emerson himself (but a very mellow Emerson by then) who, in "Historic Notes of Life and Letters in New England," called Thoreau "the only man of leisure in his town" (*C*, X, 356)!

Perhaps the best way of summarizing the matter is simply to say that Emerson, like Hawthorne's orphan-artist in "Passages from a Relinquished Work," had an Eliakim Abbott in his breast who corrected his fantasies and warned of the guilt and madness of a purely literary life. But unlike Hawthorne's hero, Emerson took the advice and read Parson Thumpcushion's letter, perhaps in the form of Sampson Reed's *Observations on the Growth of the Mind* (Emerson, when he read it in 1826, called it a "revelation"), which warned "that the end of all education is a life of active usefulness." [30] The warning, if Emerson needed one, clearly made an impression.

To be sure, as a Transcendentalist and poet, Emerson liked to envision himself a mystic—unworldly, detached, serenely inactive. In fantasy this was harmless; it was only when he was faced with it as an actual program of living that Emerson was forced to see its dangerous and illicit nature. Thus, in his position as the leading Transcendentalist of Concord, Emerson could actually think of Thoreau as an activist: "Ellery [Channing] says, that writers never do anything: they are passive observers. Some of them seem to do, but they do not; H. will

never be a writer; he is active as a shoemaker" (*J*, VI, 467–68).
Or once again:

> Henry Thoreau sports the doctrines of activity: but I say,
> What do *we*? We want a sally into the regions of wisdom, and
> do we go out and lay stone wall or dig a well or turnips? No,
> we leave the children, sit down by a fire, compose our bodies to
> corpses, shut our hands, shut our eyes, that we may be
> entranced and see truly. (*J*, VII, 521)

But when the mist disappeared from his eyes and the world
began knocking at the door to demand that Emerson be up and
doing, he could turn viciously on this image: "The State is our
neighbors; our neighbors are the State. . . . I confess I lose all
respect for this tedious denouncing of the State by idlers who
rot in indolence, selfishness, and envy in the chimney corner"
(*Ibid.*, 18). It was in such a public mood as this, when the
stern daughter of the voice of God whispered in his ear, that
Emerson would revile Thoreau for lacking ambition. Yet
Emerson might more appropriately have been envious. After
all, it was Thoreau, not he, who really had the ability to lay the
stone wall or dig the well—and Thoreau could also write.
    Inevitably, when it came to a philosophy of composition,
the radical divergence of the two men asserted itself in characteristic fashion. Emerson, abandoning his mystic separateness,
willingly altered his style to suit public taste; Thoreau, firmly
entrenched in his craft, refused to abandon his private aesthetic. Emerson wrote in *The Conduct of Life* that "the hero is
he who is immovably centred" (*C*, VI, 277). If so, Thoreau
probably considered himself qualified admirably for the title in
his dogged resistance to Emerson's varying standards. In 1853,
Emerson noted in his journal a discussion on the subject
between himself and Thoreau:

> The other day, Henry Thoreau was speaking to me about my
> lecture on the Anglo-American, and regretting that whatever

was written for a lecture, or whatever succeeded with the audience was bad, etc. I said, I am ambitious to write something which all can read, like *Robinson Crusoe*. . . . Henry objected, of course, and vaunted the better lectures which only reached a few persons.[31]

Thoreau had stated his position clearly in *A Week:* "Give me a sentence which no intelligence can understand" (*W*, I, 157). And he was to repeat himself substantially in *Walden* by insisting on *"extra vagance"* (*W*, II, 357); his goal was sublime obscurity. But Emerson disagreed. In another journal entry for 1856 he outlined his new aesthetic:

> This climate and people are a new test for the wares of a man of letters. All his thin, watery matter freezes; 'tis only the smallest portion of alcohol that remains good. At the lyceum, the stout Illinoian, after a short trial, walks out of the hall. The Committee tell you that the people want a hearty laugh, and Stark, and Saxe, and Park Benjamin, who give them that, are heard with joy. Well, I think with Governor Reynolds, the people are always right (in a sense), and that a man of letters is to say, These are the new conditions to which I must conform. . . . I must give my wisdom a comic form, instead of tragics or elegiacs, and well I know to do it. (*J*, IX, 7–8)

Fortunately, Emerson was no great believer in consistency (unlike Thoreau, who in 1841 denigrated "the fickle person . . . who has . . . a new prudence for every hour" [*W*, VII, 257]) and had apparently forgotten his journal entry of eight years previous: "Happy is he who looks only into his work to know if it will succeed, never into the times or the public opinion; and who writes from the love of imparting certain thoughts and not from the necessity of sale" (*J*, VII, 440). If "the people are always right (in a sense)," they are clearly *not* always right; how then, Thoreau might have asked, was a writer to attain purity of heart or of art by obeying their

dictates? Emerson could defend himself, of course, by implying
that although he chose to adapt himself to public
demand—thereby succeeding where Thoreau failed—he nevertheless maintained his integrity privately. But it was just this
sort of Emersonian double standard that distressed and alienated Thoreau. For him it constituted both a betrayal of art and
a personal capitulation to popular standards.

Yet Thoreau, like Hawthorne, was not unaware of the
dangers of his choice of profession and his single-minded
method of following it. He too was gnawed by doubt and guilt
and fears of being considered idle, particularly at the beginning
of his career, as in this journal passage for 1842:

> I must confess I have felt mean enough when asked how I was
> to act on society, what errand I had to mankind. Undoubtedly
> I did not feel mean without a reason, and yet my loitering is
> not without defense. I would fain communicate the wealth of
> my life to men, would really give them what is most precious
> in my gift. . . . It is hard to be a good citizen of the world in
> any great sense; but if we do render no interest or increase to
> mankind out of that talent God gave us, we can at least
> preserve the principle unimpaired. (W, VII, 350–51)

Along with Hawthorne, Thoreau was resolved, whether he
turned out a great artist or not, to be satisfied with and
scrupulous of "what his father left him." Wrongheaded as it
may have seemed finally to Emerson, Thoreau believed that
the writer must choose to be damned for the glory of his
personal gods. And he seems ultimately to have felt that
Emerson, by learning to keep an eye on popular taste, had
transferred his allegiance from the shrine of beauty to that of
prudence.

Nature as Symbol:
Emerson's Noble Doubt

I

SOME theosophists, Emerson tells us in *Nature*, "have arrived at a certain hostility and indignation towards matter, as the Manichean and Plotinus. They distrusted in themselves any looking back to these flesh-pots of Egypt. Plotinus was ashamed of his body" (C, I, 58). The gist of Emerson's argument is that philosophical idealism, which teaches that matter is only phenomenal and not substantial, led Plotinus to scorn his flesh. An enterprising psychological critic, however, might be tempted to reverse the proposition and suggest that it was Plotinus' shame which led his adoption of idealism. Emerson himself had a friend who theorized in a similar fashion: "I knew a witty physician who found the creed in the biliary duct, and used to affirm that if there was disease in the liver, the man became a Calvinist, and if that organ was sound, he became a Unitarian." [1] In like manner, the student of Emerson may fairly be led to conjecture that Emerson's temperament and emotional attitudes had more than a little to do with the development of his ideas, particularly with regard to nature and the value of sense experience. There is certainly a good deal of evidence to support such a theory.

In the first place, Emerson's professed inability to feel the weight of his experience undoubtedly made it relatively easy for him to accept a philosophy which denied the value of experience in and for itself. In his journal he often complained of his lack of emotional energy: "The capital defect of my nature for society (as it is of so many others) is the want of animal spirits. They seem to me a thing incredible, as if God should raise the dead." [2] Emerson himself apparently could not raise the dead sufficiently in his imagination to feel even the impact of death. When his son died, he wrote to Caroline Sturgis in a vein which, unless we wish to accuse Emerson of posing, is clearly a confession of a temperamental lack:

> I chiefly grieve that I cannot grieve; that this fact takes no more deep hold than other facts, is as dreamlike as they; a lambent flame that will not burn playing on the surface of my river.[3]

Commenting on this passage, Ralph Rusk suggests that Emerson "only exaggerated a fact of his nature and of his philosophy which he stated again, with like exaggeration, in the essay 'Experience.' " [4] But certainly Emerson would not have wanted to exaggerate his inability to be affected at such a time; to do so would have been to worsen the difficulty by substituting rhetoric for emotion. Moreover, with regard to "Experience," it would seem more just to remark that Emerson there exaggerated a fact of his nature *into* a philosophy. In that essay we find the admission made to Caroline Sturgis transformed in just such a fashion: "I grieve that grief can teach me nothing, nor carry me one step into real nature" (C, III, 49). If Emerson could not grieve, then the only satisfactory explanation for him must have been that grief did not exist. Yet another man, such as Henry Adams, might find grief the most impressive of educators. And Thoreau, after witnessing his brother John's horrible death by lockjaw, responded by falling dangerously ill with a sympathetic attack of the same disease, as Emerson himself relates.[5]

That Emerson's response to the death of his son is not an untypical illustration of his nature is made clear by his reaction to the death of his first wife, Ellen. In his *Life of Ralph Waldo Emerson*, Professor Rusk relates the incident in the following manner:

> He continued to complain of his lack of emotion, and when he went back "to the first smile of Ellen on the door-stone at Concord" and reviewed the whole history of his love affair with her, it was his own coolness, as he imagined it, that he regretted.[6]

We are faced once again with the simple fact that for Emerson there was an unbreachable and inexplicable discontinuity between his understanding and his emotional response. Coleridge's description of his state in "Dejection" would seem equally well to describe Emerson's reaction to his own coldness:

> I see them all so excellently fair,
> I see, not feel, how beautiful they are!

Coleridge, however, blames this painful discontinuity on a *failure* of "genial spirits," which may yet revive; Emerson seems simply to have lacked such spirits. Unlike Coleridge, who attempted to understand and correct his failure, Emerson (perplexed as he may have been from time to time) resolved the problem by elevating his own nature to the level of philosophical truth. His relative impermeability to emotional experience led to a kind of benign solipsism, such as we find in his essay "Friendship":

> I cannot deny it, O friend, that the vast shadow of the Phenomenal includes thee also in its pied and painted immensity,—thee also, compared with whom all else is shadow. Thou art not Being, as Truth is, as Justice is,—thou art not my soul, but a picture and effigy of that. (C, II, 197)

Since human contact left Emerson as it found him, the reason must have been that there was something more important— namely, truth and justice, which he identified with his omnipotent but moral ego. Yet Emerson did not really want to depeople the world. His denial of any but phenomenal being to others was not a description of the world, but rather a stratagem which at once helped to rationalize his temperament and epitomize his values. The solipsistic pose served to protect him from self-recrimination by denying the intrinsic worth of the passional experience in which he felt himself unable to participate.

Emerson's flight from experience unquestionably had its basis not only in an essentially fastidious temperament but also in a complex of conscious attitudes discernible in his earliest writings. Primarily, of course, the young Emerson owed to his Christian training a distrust of the senses and a belief in man's dualistic nature. At the age of nineteen, he wrote in his journal:

> There are two natures in man,—flesh and spirit,—whose tendencies are wide as the universe asunder, and from whose miraculous combination it arises, that he is urged alway by the visible eloquent image of Truth, toward immortal perfection, and allured aside from the painful pursuit, by gross but fascinating pleasure. (*Jn*, I, 139)

At the same time, Emerson all but declared himself a Manichean:

> They did not widely err who proclaimed the existence of two warring principles, the incorruptible mind, and the mass of malignant matter. This was a creed which was often damned as heresy by the infallible church; happy if they had never devised a worse. (*Jn*, I, 140)

Although Emerson was later to deny the absolute antipathy of Ormuzd and Ahriman (*C*, X, 213), he was never to lose the feeling that matter is malignant and that sensuous experience, though fascinating, is gross and dangerous. Probably the strongest influence on Emerson in this respect (and in many others) was his aunt Mary Moody Emerson. Cranky, well-read, and staunchly Calvinistic, she brooked no contradiction and remained, until her death in 1863, an important force in Emerson's life. In 1822 he copied a passage from one of her letters into his notebook:

> Not safe for E to explore the poor old world. The less known of it the better. Even the erudition you tax me with wanting may be beneath attention. Why use a Scaffold if the Executioner be kind enough to free you from the fleshy nook without. The material world is fine as notices of the future imperishable—as instruments of thought. (*Jn,* I, 200)

Plato, Swedenborg, and Indian thought might corroborate what Emerson received here from Aunt Mary, but they could hardly add to it substantially. Moreover, and perhaps more importantly, she undoubtedly exacerbated the distress which the young Waldo was already feeling over the contrary tendencies of flesh and spirit. If the world, as Aunt Mary warned, was indeed a snare and a delusion, perhaps it was best left alone. Emerson was finally to decide that "a world of sensations is a world of men without heads" (*J,* VI, 108), and it was an early resolution of his not to fall into that sort of idiocy (*J,* I, 167). Spenser, whose *Faerie Queene* Emerson had certainly read by 1820, had issued the same warning eloquently:

> "Let Gryll be Gryll, and have his hoggish minde;
> But let us hence depart, whilest wether serves and winde."

For Emerson willingness to depart from the world of sense experience was clearly a sign of nobility and virtue. Indeed, he was later to consider a man's attitude on the subject a perfect index of the state of his soul:

A man cannot utter two or three sentences without disclosing
to intelligent ears precisely where he stands in life and
thought, namely, whether in the kingdom of the senses and
the understanding, or in that of ideas and imagination, in the
realm of intuitions and duty. (C, VI, 224)

There was little to be hoped from a man who declared himself
at home in the world, and Emerson let it be known (at least to
himself, since he was writing in his journal) where he stood in
the matter:

My great-grandfather was Rev. Joseph Emerson of Malden,
son of Edward Emerson, Esq., of Newbury(port). I used often
to hear that when William, son of Joseph, was yet a boy
walking before his father to church, on a Sunday, his father
checked him: "William, you walk as if the earth was not good
enough for you." "I did not know it, Sir," he replied, with the
utmost humility. This is one of the household anecdotes in
which I have found a relationship. 'Tis curious, but the same
remark was made to me, by Mrs. Lucy Brown, when I walked
one day under her windows here in Concord. (J, VI, 469)

Perhaps Emerson meant here to laud William's humility and,
by extension, his own. But there is no doubt that what he really
approved of was William's attitude toward the world, and he
was greatly pleased to have Mrs. Brown say the same of him. It
was clearly a mark of distinction: the scholar, Emerson was to
remark in one of his addresses, "is too good for the world" (C,
X, 241). Thoreau, we might note in passing, took an opposite
view: he praised Chaucer because he "was not too good to
live." [7]

Unlike Thoreau, Emerson had little desire to eat a woodchuck raw or to stand up to his chin all day in a retired swamp.
Intellectually and emotionally predisposed to leave sense experience alone, this great American Romantic seems to have
made it impossible for himself to feel anything but alien to that
natural world which he recommended to his readers so drama-

tically in 1836. He recorded exactly this difficulty in a journal entry for 1838:

> I went at sundown to the top of Dr. Ripley's hill and renewed my vows to the Genius of that place. Somewhat of awe, somewhat grand and solemn mingles with the beauty that shines afar around. . . . Yet sweet and native as all those fair impressions on that summit fall on the eye and ear, they are not yet mine. I cannot tell why I should feel myself such a stranger in nature. (*J*, V, 46–47)

Having admittedly a "child's love" for nature (*C*, I, 59), however, Emerson was obviously not willing to abandon it utterly. Indeed, in 1825 he had seemed to feel that his business was to be that of the poet of nature:

> No information transmitted from one man to another can be more interesting than the accurate description of this little world in which he lies; and I shall deserve the thanks of every knowing reader, if I shall shew him the colour, orbit, and composition of my particular star. (*J*, II, 44–45)

And ten years later he outlined a program for himself that might have served as a prospectus for Thoreau's *Journal*:

> If life were long enough, among my thousand and one works should be a book of nature whereof Howitt's *Seasons* should be not so much the model as the parody. It should contain the natural history of the woods around my shifting camp for every month in the year. It should tie their astronomy, botany, physiology, meteorology, picturesque, and poetry together. No bird, no bug, no bud, should be forgotten on his day and hour. (*J*, III, 460–61)

But, as he continued his rhapsody, Emerson sounded the note which was to characterize his particular way of dealing with nature: "The river flowed brimful, and I philosophised upon this composite, collective beauty which refuses to be analysed. Nothing is beautiful alone. Nothing but is beautiful in the whole" (*Ibid.*, 461). Individual sense experience might be vain, sordid, and perhaps even dangerous; but taken altogether, the world was somehow much less formidable.

Such was to be his device for dealing with the world: he would absorb it as a whole and then reproduce it in a form closer to his heart's desire. Exactly this scheme is expressed symbolically in a dream Emerson recorded in his journal:

> I dreamed that I floated at will in the great Ether, and I saw this world floating also not far off, but diminished to the size of an apple. Then an angel took it in his hand and brought it to me and said, "This must thou eat." And I ate the world.[8]

Emerson's task seems almost to have divine sanction—the sad task of swallowing the bitter fruit of worldly knowledge. Still, it was better to take the world this way, rather than piece by piece in daily experience. Emerson's dream both epitomizes his problem and suggests a solution. Having obliterated the world as matter, this "young god making experiments in creation" [9] could then give it all back as pure idea.

In characteristic fashion, then, Emerson simply dealt with the natural world the way he did with anything, such as grief or evil, that displeased him: he refused to believe in its existence. To be sure, there might be something of egotism in this; Emerson often felt that he was too good for the world. But he was also a man unequivocally in love with the beautiful and the good. If the world of the senses, which for most people is the real and the existent, seemed to him sordid, what solution was there except to say that the beautiful could not possibly exist in the same fashion? As Emerson remarked to a friend one day while on a walk to Walden, "I declare this world is so beautiful that I can hardly believe it exists" (*J*, V, 382). But, as Emerson was aware, his stratagem was liable to lay him open to the charge of not really being a lover of the created universe. He would insist otherwise:

I have no hatred to the round earth and its gray mountains. I see well enough the sand-hill opposite my window. I see with as much pleasure as another a field of corn or a rich pasture, whilst I dispute their absolute being. Their phenomenal being I no more dispute than I do my own. I do not dispute, but point out the just way of viewing them. (*J*, IV, 12)

Yet, unfortunately, Emerson's just way of viewing the world was primarily a personal stratagem and only secondarily a metaphysical position, and the acrimony of dispute was built into his Ideal theory. As he asserted in *Nature*, the doubt of the existence of matter is "noble," while the opposite view is "vulgar" and held only by the unregenerate—those who, having an "unrenewed understanding," are addicted to the senses, which are "low" (C, I, 47, 59, 49, 12). A belief in idealism seems almost a sign of election, or at least an indication of good breeding, as this journal entry suggests:

To the rude it seems as if matter had absolute existence, existed from an intrinsic necessity. The first effect of thought is to make us sensible that spirit exists from an intrinsic necessity, that matter has a merely phenomenal or accidental being, being created from spirit, or being the manifestation of spirit. (*J*, IV, 13)

For Emerson the Ideal theory was the emperor's new clothes of Transcendentalism—a touchstone for testing one's taste and discretion. Anyone who dared say that the emperor had nothing on was rude and would merit being ostracized from the Transcendental court.

II

Emerson was driven to accept the Ideal theory because he found sense experience distasteful, not because he really believed that the world was an illusion. Convinced by temperament and training that the mind and the body, the spirit and nature, were not only separate but unequal—that the soul was higher, finer, and truer than matter—he needed a theory, other than Christianity, that would bestow intellectual dignity upon these sentiments. Idealism was the answer. It would serve the double purpose of presenting Emerson as the humble prophet of a new religion, while at the same time implying his aristocratic spirit. By applying the Ideal theory to nature, he could justify his fastidious tastes on the grounds of a seemingly Romantic philosophy and perhaps even prove ultimately that he was a better citizen than most people thought. But an avowal of idealism also had its dangers: the taint of otherworldliness, with its damning implications of "Orientalism" and "moonshine"; the horrors of skepticism (as Emerson once put it, the "slow suicide" of a Schopenhauer); and finally the possibility of hypocrisy, since Puritan times a besetting sin of the Protestant world view.

An early and highly important influence on Emerson, Dr. Richard Price, in his *Review of the Principal Questions and Difficulties in Morals,* had used the same *ad hominem* argument that Emerson was to employ in defending a qualified idealism. Price quoted Plato to ridicule those who deny what they cannot sense: ". . . those who have not learnt to look above all sensibles and individuals to abstract truth and the natures of things, to beauty or good itself, are not to be ranked amongst true philosophers, but among the ignorant, the vulgar, and blind." But Price went on to deplore the fact that what Plato "delivered to this purpose has been carried into mysticism and jargon, by the *latter Platonists;* but this is no reason for rejecting it." [10] Idealism, then, when it led to a satisfactory ethical position, was permissible and desirable; but when it carried its devotee off to lonely mystic contemplation, it became nonsense and jargon. In similar fashion, although Emerson had only contempt for "the broker, the wheelwright, the carpenter, the tollman" (C, I, 49)—those too imbruted to understand that nature, in Yeats's words, is "but a spume that plays/Upon a ghostly paradigm of things"—he certainly had no use for an Ideal theory that ended in mysticism:

> It is essential to a true theory of nature and of man, that it should contain somewhat progressive. Uses that are exhausted or that may be, and facts that end in the statement, cannot be all that is true of this brave lodging wherein man is harbored, and wherein all his faculties find appropriate and endless exercise.
>
> . . . when a faithful thinker, resolute to detach every object from personal relations and see it in the light of thought, shall, at the same time, kindle science with the fire of the holiest affections, then will God go forth anew into the creation. (C, I, 61, 74)

For Emerson, idealism was meant to strengthen the backbone of nineteenth-century youths by turning them from pleasure to pious performance. The lotus, as a food or as a position, was not being recommended.

As for the dangerous skepticism implied in a thoroughgoing idealism, Dr. Price had dealt with that too:

> . . . it is *self-evident,* that a *material world,* answerable to our ideas, and to what we feel and see, is *possible.* We have no reason to think that it does not exist. Every thing appears as if it did exist; and against the reality of its existence there is nothing but a bare possibility against actual feeling, and all the evidence which our circumstances and condition, as embodied spirits, seem capable of . . . the same principles on which the existence of *matter* is opposed, lead us equally to deny the existence of *spiritual* beings.[11]

Once begin to doubt the faculties, Price asserted, and there would be no end to confusion. For him idealism simply implied the existence of absolute truth, capable of being intuited by the human mind. Matter too he considered an intuition of the mind, but one of lesser value. Thus Price avoided the possible problem of the dualism of mind and matter inherent in idealism by resolutely ignoring the puzzles of epistemology. The promptings of spirit and the promptings of matter are equally real, but the spirit is better. Emerson ultimately ended up in the same position, but he did—perhaps unfortunately— broach the epistemological problem in his desire to win converts from matter to spirit. In the end, of course, he attempted to resolve the problem, but simply by a strategy of self-reliance, not in any philosophically rigorous fashion.

Emerson, like Price, had no use for skepticism when it threatened his argument: "The frivolous make themselves merry with the Ideal theory, as if its consequences were burlesque; as if it affected the stability of nature. It surely does not" (C, I, 48). Yet Emerson's idealism, on its ontological side, did seem to affect the stability of matter, as it questioned the reliability of perception on its epistemological side. Emerson himself never tired of saying that matter is accidental, and this clearly tends to cast doubt on its stability. But, in fact, Emerson never really meant to question the stability of nature; it was its intrinsic value he doubted.

In his zeal, however, to "put nature under foot" (Ibid., 58), he unfortunately seemed to will it out of existence. He did this by resolving the problem of epistemological dualism much to the disadvantage of nature. Faced with the disparity between perception and the thing perceived, he decided that the instability lay in nature rather than in the mind of the beholder.[12] Clearly, if the world of perception is the "true" one, then the so-called "real" world is phenomenal, a shifting dream which cannot be trusted. Having established that perception is the supreme arbiter of reality—that the mind is the true guide to knowledge—Emerson used this argument to resolve the problem of psycho-physical dualism in favor of "mental" entities. "Ideas" (such as truth, goodness, and justice) he considered to be the only real existents, having their home in the mind of the noble doubter; "things" he considered to be mere appearances—shadows and symbols, perhaps, of divine truth but worthless in themselves.

Once he had established that the intuitions of a noble soul have precedence, as truth, over sense experience, Emerson was quite willing to allow the world to go on existing. His aim had been to resolve, without Christianity, the Christian dualism between flesh and spirit in favor of spirit, and to this end he happily pre-empted the arguments of a skeptical solipsist. But he balked at the dangerous conclusions of the latter:

> Yet, if it [idealism] only deny the existence of matter, it does not satisfy the demands of the spirit. It leaves God out of me. It leaves me in the splendid labyrinth of my perceptions, to wander without end. (C, I, 63)

We should note that for Emerson skepticism is bad, not because it leaves God out of the universe, but because it leaves God out of man. It denies self-reliance, which for Emerson is God-reliance, since God—the moral law—resides in man. But Emerson had solved the problem before stating it by simply asserting, in the manner of an arrogant Descartes, the epistemological and ontological stability of man's spirit: I think truth, therefore I am true. So that idealism, for Emerson, ends up "merely as a useful introductory hypothesis, serving to apprize us of the eternal distinction between the soul and the world" (*Ibid.*). The noble doubt should serve to inspire self-reverence and a belief in "ideas," not universal uncertainty.

Interestingly, the "labyrinth" passage from *Nature* is almost certainly an adaptation of a passage from William Drummond's *Academical Questions* which Emerson had found in *The Edinburgh Review* in 1820 and copied into his notebook. The selection from Drummond is pretty clearly a Lockean slap at idealism:

We forget our first impressions; nor recollect how simple are
the elements of all our knowledge. Deluded by his own mind
man continues to wander in the mazes of the labyrinth which
lies before him, unsuspicious of his deviations from the truth.
Like some Knight of romance in an enchanted palace he
mistakes the fictitious for the real & the false for the true. (*Jn*,
I, 376)

Emerson, however, liked his labyrinth; it was, in fact, "splen-
did." Only God was missing; so he drew Him in and transformed *Nature* from a palpably ethical tract into one religious
at least in terminology. As for Drummond's suggestion that all
knowledge begins with sense experience, Emerson would have
none of it. Indeed, what need did he have of knowledge at all,
since (to paraphrase Santayana on Kant) he had come to
remove knowledge in order to make room for faith? The
sensuous philosophy was barbaric and perhaps even infantile:
"Children, it is true, believe in the external world. The belief
that it appears only, is an afterthought, but with culture this
faith will as surely arise on the mind as did the first" (*C*, I, 59).
If children believe that the world is real, they had best be seen
and not heard, until experience has taught them that experience is vain and delusive. But it was hard for a professed
Romantic and lover of the "Ode: On Intimations of Immortality . . ." to be thus severe with the youngsters. So, inconse-
quently, Emerson ended his essay by offering "the wisdom of
children" as one example of "Reason's momentary grasp of the
sceptre" (*Ibid.*, 73).

Perhaps there was no real inconsistency, however, in Emerson's attitude toward "the wisdom of children." Looked at from
one side, he simply used the argument of an adult—idealism—
to justify what he considered to be the child's natural position:
worldly innocence. Conversely, starting with a belief in innocence and temperance, he worked his way up to a theory
which, though metaphysically extreme, seemed to embody

those values. In the first instance, children were wrong only because they did not know enough to use a sophisticated argument to defend their position. But the argument could be dispensed with once the position was reached.

Emerson may have felt that he had overstated his case in *Nature*, where he had simply used a metaphysical theory to support an ethical position: idealism was only a metaphor for a call to worldly asceticism. At any rate, he had to reinstate the world. In "The Conservative," which he delivered in 1841, he stated the case strongly: ". . . the existing world is not a dream, and cannot with impunity be treated as a dream; neither is it a disease; but it is the ground on which you stand, it is the mother of whom you were born" (*C*, I, 303). If Emerson felt that he had come to be known as the man who said that the world is a dream (and he had implied just that in *Nature*), then it was high time to correct the impression before his friends and his own conscience began to cry hypocrite:

> An idealist, if he have the sensibilities and habits of those whom I know, is very ungrateful. He craves and enjoys every chemical property, and every elemental force, loves pure air, water, light, caloric, wheat, flesh, salt, and sugar; the blood coursing in his own veins, and the grasp of friendly hands; and uses the meat he eats to preach against matter as malignant, and to praise mind, which he very hollowly and treacherously serves. Beware of hypocrisy. (*J*, IX, 6)

Emerson's own analysis here of what he was about is probably more astute than anything the student can hope to come up with.

This journal entry was made in 1856, but the problem was a constant one for Emerson: Must the spiritual man completely renounce the world? If he does not, has he ceased to serve mind? Emerson knew well enough that the world was real. Was he a refined materialist who justified his fastidiousness by posing as an idealist? Perhaps he was being too hard on himself; everyone, including Emerson himself, knew that he was not self-seeking. One thing at least was clear: he preached not against matter absolutely, but against matter as an end in itself, a sensual trap. Matter as the stuff of duty was fine. If this was materialism, it was certainly of an exalted kind. That it was not idealism, strictly speaking, was beside the point; only a philosopher would argue about terminology.

If the knowledge that he was not really otherworldly made Emerson feel hypocritical in his position as an idealist, he could at least content himself with the realization that his use of the world had never been selfish. He preached abnegation, not self-indulgence. This, at heart, was the burden of his idealism: man's business was to serve the absolute. And if this absolute turned out to be not some Platonic idea, but his own society, so much the better:

> What a debt is ours to that old religion which, in the childhood of most of us, still dwelt like a sabbath morning in the country of New England, teaching privation, self-denial and sorrow! A man was born not for prosperity, but to suffer for the benefit of others, like the noble rock-maple which all around our villages bleeds for the service of man. (C, I, 220)

Here, in "The Method of Nature" (1841), Emerson urged his listeners "to bewail [their] innocency and to recover it, and with it the power to communicate again with these sharers of a more sacred idea" (Ibid.). His theme was the same as that of Carlyle's Sartor Resartus and his own Nature: man's end is not to be happy, but to do his work. Emerson tried to "woo and court" his readers "from every object in nature, from every fact in life, from every thought in the mind," to the notion that "the one condition coupled with the gift of truth is its use" (Ibid., 222). Carlyle had translated "Know thyself" into "Know what thou canst work at"; Emerson transformed the ancient maxim into "Study nature." But was there really any difference between the two, since for Emerson nature was the stepping-stone to virtuous action? The real value of nature lay not in details, not in the low and mediate pleasures of the five senses, but in the moral teachings which he found embodied in nature as a whole. His idealism, therefore, was simply a way of saying that natural phenomena as *existents* were not really important. Nature had a higher use, as man had a higher duty, than mere sensuous pleasure.

/ Auxiliary

III

It is a curiosity of nineteenth-century literary and intellectual history that Emerson has earned the reputation of being a Romantic despite the fact that his major doctrine amounts unmistakably to a belief in the beautiful necessity of worshipping the human conscience.[13] In Emerson's view, nature is completely ancillary to moral science and is best used when it serves to furnish rhetorical tropes with which to adorn a discourse. The business of the poet, as of the preacher and the scientist, is "to hunt out and to exhibit the analogies between moral and material nature in such a manner as to have a bearing upon practice" (*J*, II, 241–42). Nor, it might be suggested, was Emerson a typologist of nature, either in the literal fashion of an Origen—whose "extravagances" Emerson condemned outright in his journal (*J*, II, 25)—or, more importantly, in the mystical fashion of Jonathan Edwards, who saw nature as intrinsically valuable and true.[14] For Emerson "every natural fact is trivial until it becomes symbolical or moral" (*J*, V, 421). And:

> Whilst common sense looks at things or visible Nature as real and final facts, poetry, or the imagination which dictates it, is a second sight, looking through these, and using them as types or words for thoughts which they signify. (*C*, VIII, 19)

Unlike Edwards, who, as Perry Miller tells us, quoted "Scripture to confirm the meaning of natural phenomena," [15] Emerson argued from nature to Scripture: "All things with which we deal, preach to us. What is a farm but a mute gospel?" (C, I, 42). And, again unlike Edwards, Emerson had small use for that art which amounted to no more than an imitation or description of nature, since he considered the latter to be intrinsically of little value.[16] Emerson, for example, continually criticized Wordsworth for being "foolishly inquisitive about the essence and body of what pleased him, of what all sensible men feel to be, in its nature, evanescent" (J, II, 108–9); and although the youthful desire to "abuse" Wordsworth which is apparent in the following early journal entry (1819) was to disappear, Emerson's attitude toward "nature in poetry" would not change substantially:

> He is the poet of pismires. His inspirations are spent light. It is one of the greatest mistakes in the [world] to suppose that that much abused virtue of nature in poetry consists in mere fidelity of representation. (Jn, I, 162)

Emerson had a different view, namely, that nature should be touched "gently, as illustration or ornament. Beds of flowers send up a most grateful scent to the passenger who hastens by them, but let him pitch his tent among them and he will find himself grown insensible to their fragrance" (J, II, 232). Emerson had no desire to glut his sorrow on a rose or die of it in aromatic pain; a quick whiff of the moral law was really what he wanted from the natural world, rather than a moment of sublime illumination. Unlike Edwards, who was a religious phenomenologist, Emerson was a pious Platonist who went to nature for confirmation and illustration of his a priori ethical system, not for mystic ecstasy inseparable from its ineffable meaning.

Emerson, in fact, thought he knew perfectly well what

nature meant and devoted his *Nature* to an assertion of that meaning. Indeed, Emerson's own sad admission that there was a "crack" in his first book between the chapters on "Discipline" and "Idealism" may appear to be overly harsh self-criticism to a reader who has come to terms with what Emerson's idealism really signifies—a simple denial of the inherent worth of matter and sense experience. All of *Nature* has one theme, and there is actually no disparity among its sections. In the chapter on "Commodity," for instance, we learn that "a man is fed, not that he may be fed, but that he may work" (*C, I, 14*). Nature serves to enable man to do his duty, not to allow him to rest slothfully in his pleasure. Nor does the section on "Beauty" contradict this stern dictum, although Emerson seems to suggest that aesthetic satisfaction is an end in itself when he states that "the world . . . exists to the soul to satisfy the desire of beauty. This element I call an ultimate end." He quickly adds the warning that "beauty in nature is not ultimate" (*Ibid.*, 24). Virtue, we realize, is what beauty really exists to imply. In the next section we find that language serves as the medium of expression for parables of moral truth, while nature functions as the symbol of spirit, which equals the human mind, which in turn implies ethical awareness. This reading is made explicit in the chapter on "Discipline," where Emerson tells us that "sensible objects conform to the premonitions of Reason and reflect the conscience." Things "hint or thunder to man the laws of right and wrong, and echo the Ten Commandments," and "the moral law lies at the centre of nature" (*Ibid.*, 40–41).

The connection between the sections on "Discipline" and "Idealism" is, then, by no means obscure if we consider that to a man enamored of his conscience, natural phenomena are indeed unimportant. Nature, which embodied Fichtean duty earlier in the essay, was scarcely real in a way which would be meaningful to a naturalist, scientist, or artist. It is therefore hardly inconsistent for Emerson to suggest that nature is less substantial, less meaningful than "ideas"—by which he means not mere abstractions and disembodied essences, but Hegelian "concrete universals," such as truth and justice, incarnated in religion and ethics, church and state:

> Whilst we behold unveiled the nature of Justice and Truth, we learn the difference between the absolute and the conditional or relative. We apprehend the absolute. As it were, for the first time, *we exist*. We become immortal, for we learn that time and space are relations of matter; that with a perception of truth or a virtuous will they have no affinity. (*Ibid.*, 57)

Emerson's idealism, then, is simply an affirmation of the supreme importance of the moral law and a restatement of the notion, expressed earlier in his essay, that nature exists (or ceases to exist) as a discipline in ethics. The essentially mundane nature of Emerson's idealism is perhaps made clearer in "Circles":

> There are degrees in idealism. We learn first to play with it academically, as the magnet was once a toy. Then we see in the heyday of youth and poetry that it may be true, that it is true in gleams and fragments. Then its countenance waxes stern and grand, and we see that it must be true. It now shows itself ethical and practical. We learn that God *is*; that he is in me; and that all things are shadows of him. The idealism of Berkeley is only a crude statement of the idealism of Jesus, and that again is a crude statement of the fact that all nature is the rapid efflux of goodness executing and organizing itself. (*C*, II, 309–10)

God is clearly the conscience, which is certainly practical and efficient when it organizes the natural world in the service of an ordered society. Idealism, to return to *Nature*, "presents the world in precisely that view which is most desirable to the mind" (*C*, I, 59)—to the mind, we should add, of the moralist, for whom ethics is infinitely more important than sensuous experience. "For seen in the light of thought, the world always is phenomenal; and virtue subordinates it to the mind" (*Ibid.*, 60). Crickets and crab apples are a distraction to a man in love with the moral law and, for him, may be said not to exist.

This theme of *Nature* is repeated almost exactly in Emerson's "Poetry and Imagination"; but there, as if to avoid from the start the seeming "moonshine" of *Nature*, Emerson commenced with a solid assertion of the existence of the world:

> The restraining grace of common sense is the mark of all the valid minds. . . . The common sense which does not meddle with the absolute, but takes things at their word,—things as they appear,—believes in the existence of matter, not because we can touch it or conceive of it, but because it agrees with ourselves, and the universe does not jest with us, but is in earnest, is the house of health and life. (*C*, VIII, 3)

Now it seems clearly nobler to believe in matter. However, Emerson has by no means become reconciled to matter in itself: "The primary use of a fact is low; the secondary use, as it is a figure or illustration of my thought, is the real worth" (*Ibid.*, 11). Nature simply serves as a source of tropes for the discourses of the moralist or, in this case, <u>the poet (who turns out to be a moralist in disguise)</u>. Emerson then returns to his idealistic strategy, but this time obliquely:

> This belief that the higher use of the material world is to furnish us types or pictures to express the thoughts of the mind, is carried to its logical extreme by the Hindoos, who, following Buddha, have made it the central doctrine of their religion that what we call Nature, the external world, has no real existence,—is only phenomenal. (*Ibid.*, 14)

"Logical extreme" may strike us as strange until we remember that idealism, at least in Boston and Concord, was "ethical and practical" and, far from having the immobilizing effect found in the East, was being approved by Emerson for the opposite reason. At any rate, if idealism as a doctrine still seemed odd to Emerson's readers, it could be blamed on Buddha rather than on the writer. Emerson then made the characteristic leap to "symbolic nature," but this time with an interesting twist: "The poet discovers that what men value as substances have a higher value as symbols; that Nature is the immense shadow of man" (*Ibid.*, 23). Previously, nature had been symbolic of spirit; but the careful reader found out that spirit was equivalent to God, and God simply a way of talking about conscience. So nature is described here as the reflection of man's moral sense—which, by a characteristic kind of synecdoche that tells us much about his views, is certainly what Emerson means by "man." Furthermore, Emerson is quick to head off the dangers of egotism and subjectivity by defining his man:

> Of course, when we describe man as poet, and credit him with the triumphs of the art, we speak of the potential or ideal man,—not found now in any one person. . . . He is the healthy, the wise, the fundamental, the manly man . . . (*Ibid.*, 26)

Like Hegel's "absolute self," Emerson's poet is a universal and not a particular man; this is an important qualification, at least for Emerson's argument, since he would appear to be unlike most poets the world has seen. Indeed, the poet soon reveals himself to be a moralist at heart, as Emerson implies when he quotes Ben Jonson: " 'The principal end of poetry is to inform men in the just reason of living' " (*Ibid.*, 38). Furthermore, the work of this man will be inspiriting, affirmative, and ethical (*Ibid.*, 64); his poetry will be "the high poetry which shall thrill and agitate mankind, restore youth and health, dissipate the dreams under which men reel and stagger, and bring in the new thoughts, the sanity and heroic aims of nations" (*Ibid.*, 73). The poet must be a moralist, for whom nature is a discipline in moral truth. Clearly, then, the sensuous experience of real nature is ruled out; it is simply too conducive to reeling and staggering.

In 1849, Emerson attempted to define the modern era in a journal entry which, perhaps better than anything else, helps us to summarize his attitude toward idealism and the true function of nature:

> *The Modern:* When the too idealistic tendencies of the Christian period running into the diseases of cant, monachism, and a church, demonstrating the impossibility of Christianity, have forced men to retrace their steps, and rally again on Nature; but now the tendency is to marry mind to Nature, and to put Nature under the mind, convert the world into the instrument of Right Reason. Man goes forth to the dominion of the world by commerce, by science, and by philosophy. (*J*, VIII, 78)

Nature is certainly substantial here, yet it hardly seems important in detail. Communion and ecstasy are replaced by progress, and art finds no honored place beside commerce, science, and philosophy. Instructed by such a passage, and bearing in mind that for Emerson "poetry and prudence should be coincident" (*C*, II, 231), the student may notice that *Nature* ends as a hymn to progress under the moral law. It predicts the "kingdom of man over nature" (*C*, I, 77), rather than the perfection of man in himself through a renewed contact with the physical world.

A naturalist might say that nature, viewed as Emerson views it in that essay, is not nature at all; and an artist might object that sense experience is intrinsically important to his life and craft. But for Emerson, who ultimately cared less for sense experience than for public morality, his theory of nature was a strategy of self-justification which his neighbors could understand. Nature as symbol was the kind of "Romanticism" that New England had lived with since its founding.

CHAPTER FOUR

The Moral Law:

Emerson's Cosmic Vision

I

EMERSON nowhere shows greater affinity to the eighteenth century than in his firm belief in the "moral sense," or "moral sentiment," or "Moral Law." And nothing more amazingly exhibits what small effect, at heart, a lifetime of reading his European contemporaries had on his ideas. In this sense at least, one might say that Emerson never developed at all. Indeed, when writing to his Aunt Mary on this subject in 1841, he put himself clearly in the position of a Unitarian—a child of the Enlightenment—trying to convince a Calvinist that some common ground still remained between them: ". . . we should meet where truly we are at one in our perception of one Law in our adoration of the Moral sentiment." [1]

According to Ralph Rusk, Emerson's introduction to this idea is probably traceable to his having studied at Harvard under Levi Frisbie and Levi Hedge, both of whom "followed Dugald Stewart and Thomas Brown in protesting against Locke and Paley":

> So far as Frisbie and Hedge represented the college, its teaching was an endorsement of the Edinburgh brand of Scottish philosophy and pointed slightly in the direction of Transcendentalism. The refurbishing of what was essentially

the outmoded Shaftesbury-Hutcheson theory of the moral
sense was a feature that Ralph Emerson would certainly not
soon forget.[2]

A close student of this problem, Merrell Davis, while admitting
that Emerson got his terminology from Coleridge, argues that
Emerson found the idea of the Transcendental "Reason" in
Dugald Stewart:

> Stewart's discussion of the moral sense is in its basic tenets the
> same as that which Emerson expressed in his *Journals* for
> 1822, a year after we know that he had been reading Stewart's
> analysis. It is thus reasonable to assert that Emerson was
> familiar with the idea of an intuitive moral faculty, "coeval
> with the first operations of the intellect," from his reading and
> study of Stewart during the last years of his undergraduate
> days at Harvard.[3]

While it is probably true that Emerson found the *term* "moral
sense"—with the connotation he later attached to "Reason"—
in his reading of Stewart, the idea behind the term is clearly
traceable to an earlier source, one which helps place the genesis
of Emerson's ideas much more squarely in that deistic eighteenth century which he is supposed to have repudiated thoroughly. This earlier source is the English Unitarian Richard
Price, whose theories, according to Sir Leslie Stephen, were
"chiefly a reproduction of the old optimistic Deism of Clarke
and Wollaston," blended with a touch of Bishop Butler.[4] Price
did not, of course, use the term *moral sense;* he avoided it in
order to differentiate his theories (not really successfully, as we
shall see) from those of Francis Hutcheson. But the term itself
is hardly important. Emerson used it interchangeably with
"moral sentiment" and "Moral Law," and he obviously always
meant the same thing by it.

In all likelihood, Emerson received his first impetus to read

Price from his Aunt Mary. To be sure, she made it clear that he had invented nothing new in morals and was simply stating principles that were eternal; but she obviously approved of Price as suitable reading for the seventeen-year-old Waldo.[5]

Emerson's first journal entry on Price's *Review of the Principal Questions and Difficulties in Morals* is dated March 14, 1821 (nearly a full year before his first mention of Stewart):

> I am reading Price on Morals & intend to read it with care & commentary. I shall set down here what remarks occur to me upon the matter or manner of his argument. On the 56 Page Dr Price says that right & wrong are not determined by any reasoning or deduction but by an ultimate perception of the human mind. It is to be desired that this were capable of satisfactory proof but (as it) is in direct opposition to the skeptical philosophy it cannot stand unsupported by strong & sufficient evidence. I will however read more & see if it is proved or no.—He saith that the Understanding is this ultimate determiner. (*Jn*, I, 51)

As the editors of the 1960 edition of Emerson's *Journals* point out, the phrase given by Emerson as "an ultimate perception of the human mind" is really, in Price, "some *immediate* power of perception" (*Ibid.*). But Emerson's instinct is good: it does not take Price long to declare that "morality is *eternal and immutable.*" [6] As for the "strong and sufficient evidence" that the critical young moralist hoped to find, it never materializes in Price's book, but that can hardly be expected to have weakened Emerson's faith in Price's conclusions. Hume and Kant notwithstanding, Emerson was never a skeptic in morals. Price remained for him "one of the ablest champions of truth" (*Jn*, I, 260).

The important principle which Emerson found fully expounded in Price's *Review* we find outlined in another journal entry:

The moral /sense/faculty/? or as others term it the decision [Vide Price on Morals] of the understanding is recognized as an Original principle of our nature[,] the *intuition*(?) by which we directly determine the merit or demerit of an action. (*Jn*, I, 262)

Here Emerson's interpretation is based squarely on a correct reading of Price; and the necessary equation is established between "understanding" (later, of course, to be "Reason") and "intuition" (or, as Price has it, "a power of immediate perception, giving rise to new original ideas" [7]). In the Pricean vocabulary, of course, and in opposition to Locke, the standard separation of the mind into the "faculties" of the old psychology precedes this definition of "intuition." That is, Price first distinguishes between "sense" and "understanding"; he then splits the latter up into "reason," which has to do with deduction, and "intuition," the higher, active power of the mind. Price states that he will limit his use of "understanding" to "intuition," which is "that in the soul to which belongs . . . the apprehension of TRUTH." [8]

Another feature of Price's argument—one that finds its way into Emerson's writings variously as "bias," "whim," and "instinct"—is what Price refers to as our "instinctive determinations." Initially Price attacks Hutcheson's "moral sense" because it denies inherent rightness in ideas and makes the rightness of an idea or action a function of the impression it makes on us. This impugns the immutability and eternality of truth. Price, however, having declared that "morality is *eternal and immutable*" and invariably intuited so by the "understanding," is free to fit the "instinctive determinations" into his scheme: "How wisely then has our Maker . . . enforced our intellectual perceptions by a sense; so that now, what appears worthy and right, has a positive determination of our natures in its favour." [9] Virtue is not right because it pleases us, but pleases us because it is right. However, as Hutcheson himself insists, we can never be pleased wrongly;[10] so that, practically speaking, Price really does agree with Hutcheson's "moral sense." Price actually admits as much: " . . . to every rational mind properly disposed, morally good actions must for ever be *acceptable, and can never of themselves* offend; and morally evil actions must for ever be *disagreeable,* and can never *of themselves* please." [11] The importance of this discussion for the student of Emerson is simply that it links together "instinct," "intuition," and the "understanding" (Transcendental "Reason"). They all point infallibly to the imperative dictates of the moral law.

When we explore the nature of the law which, for Price, the "understanding" intuits, we find an interesting adumbration of the way in which theology finally gets swallowed up in ethics—but, curiously, in an ethics which, thanks to the reflected light of religion, carries with it all the supernatural sanctions of the latter. This is, of course, what happens when Emerson postulates the concept of an "Over-Soul" which sounds a good deal like the traditional Judeo-Christian God and yet manages to lose God along the way. Price writes in his *Review:*

> Morality has been represented as necessary and immutable. There is an objection to this, which to some has appeared of considerable weight, and which it will be proper for me to examine.
>
> It may seem "that this is setting up something distinct from God, which is independent of him, and equally eternal and necessary." [12]

Price's next step is to state that "morality is a branch of *necessary truth*" and that "truth and morality should stand and fall together." [13] He then adds that "to conceive of truth as depending on God's will, is to conceive of his intelligence and knowledge as depending on his will." [14] But this is preposterous, says Price, since in actuality God's will is regulated by His understanding (as, we might add, is the will of any reasonable eighteenth-century Englishman, whom God begins to resemble). Price then argues that truth is a view, mode, or attribute of God's nature, which is distinct from His will. Since Price has defined "understanding" as that which apprehends absolute truth, God's "nature" (eternal mind and eternal truth) is equivalent to His "understanding." But man, too, has the faculty of "understanding," which enables him immediately and intuitively to participate in this eternal mind. Thus man's "understanding" and "God" (God as eternal truth rather than eternal will) have deftly come together. Price concludes this part of his argument by suggesting that space and duration belong to the same category as truth. If we keep in mind the dictum that truth and morality are one, we see the way prepared for Emerson's important misreading of Kant.

The idea of the moral law as developed by Price finds its way, early and late, into Emerson's writings. The following is a journal entry for 1822:

> Moral Sense: a rule coextensive and coeval with Mind. It derives its existence from the eternal character of the Deity . . . and seems of itself to imply, and therefore to prove his Existence. . . . Whence comes this strong universal feeling that approves or abhors actions? Manifestly not from *matter*, which is altogether unmoved by it, and the connection of which with it is a thing absurd—but from *Mind*, of which it is the essence. That mind is God.
>
> This Sentiment which we bear within us, is so subtle and unearthly in its nature, so entirely distinct from all sense matter, and hence so difficult to be examined, and withal so decisive and invariable in its dictates—that it clearly partakes of another world than this, and looks forward to it in the end. . . . This Sentiment differs from the affections of the heart and from the faculties of the mind. The affections are undiscriminating and capricious. The Moral Sense is not. (J, I, 186–87)

Here the absolute nature of the moral sense is stressed, but it still partakes of the religious and is tinged with otherworldliness. By 1834 Emerson is able to say: "Blessed is the day when the youth discovers that Within and Above are synonyms" (*J*, III, 399). And in "The Over-Soul" (1841) we find "Within" and "Above" meeting in the moral law:

> We distinguish the announcements of the soul, its manifestations of its own nature, by the term *Revelation*. These are always attended by the emotion of the sublime. For this communication is an influx of the Divine mind into our mind. It is an ebb of the individual rivulet before the flowing surges of the sea of life . . . these revelations . . . are perceptions of the absolute law. (*C*, II, 280–82)

In journal entries during the 1860's the identification of truth and morality is clear:

> All the victories of religion belong to the moral sentiment. . . . The parson calls it Justification by Faith. . . . We say there exists a Universal Mind which imparts this perception of duty, opens the interior world to the humble obeyer. (*J*, X, 99–100)

> The soul, as it obeys the inward law, reveres it, comes to feel that the listening after any saint or prophet were an impiety against this immediate revelation. . . . The moral sentiment . . . is absolute and in every individual the law of the world. (*Ibid.*, 192–93)

It is important, finally, to note that in Emersonian terms the moral sentiment, moral law, and moral sense are equivalent to the revelations of the Over-Soul, to duty, and to the law of the world. Man, in his best moments, finds himself at one with the universe, and the great revelation which rises spontaneously in his soul proves to be quite simply the difference between right and wrong. For Emerson the moral sense—man's highest faculty of perception ("that sovereign sense") and his only "perfectly spiritual" part—"marshals before its divine tribunal" at once "the motives of action, the secrets of character and the interests of the universe" (*J*, I, 164).

Emerson's early formulations of the moral law show him to be surprisingly close to the eighteenth-century philosophers he is supposed to have disdained. For instance, the Hutchesonian doctrine of the "moral sense," with which, as we have noted, Price was essentially in agreement, appears substantially in a journal entry for 1822:

> . . . the Moral Law: It is not necessary to describe that law, otherwise than by saying that it is the sovereign necessity which commands every mind to abide by one mode of conduct and to reject another, by joining to the one a perfect satisfaction, while it pursues the other with indefinite apprehension. (*J*, I, 162)

Furthermore, the relation of education to the moral sense—an odd relation, since by definition the sense is intuitive—bothered Emerson (as it did Price before him [15]): "Every man /becomes/grows/ acquainted with the moral laws which govern his condition, as he does with the decencies of society—only by a growing familiarity with the order of the scene wherein he plays a part" (*Jn*, I, 87). This is perilously close to Locke, and by 1826 Emerson has attempted to move away from empiricism:

> It is an important observation that though our perception of moral truth is instinctive, and we do not owe to education our approbation of truth or our abhorrence of ingratitude, yet we are not born to any image of perfect virtue. . . . We need a learned experience to enumerate all the particulars that make the whole of virtue. (*J*, II, 89–90)

But in the same year, while eagerly reading Sampson Reed's *Observations on the Growth of the Mind*, Emerson undoubtedly noticed Reed's comments on Locke's *tabula rasa*: "There prevails a most erroneous sentiment, that the mind is originally vacant, and requires only to be filled up." [16] The problem, therefore, of the function of education in aiding "our perception of moral truth" was to be solved by redefining education, which Emerson did in a journal entry for 1831: "Education is the drawing out of the soul" (J, II, 412; cf. J, III, 416).

But once we rule out experience as the source of moral truth and declare that for each individual "a voice within speaks," [17] we are faced with the difficulty of finding sanctions for the moral truths inculcated by Price's "understanding." Price himself solves the problem by simply appealing to the "common notions" which, he believed, lie in the bosom of every man:

> It cannot be shewn that there have ever been any human beings who have had no ideas of property and justice, of the rectitude of veracity, gratitude, benevolence, prudence, and religious worship. All the difference has been about particular usages and practices, of which it is impossible but different persons must have different ideas, according to the various opinions they entertain of their relation to the universally acknowledged moral principles. [18]

Price then adds that whenever mistakes have been made, "speculative errors" will be found. Cannibals must know that eating people is wrong; they simply choose to ignore the invariable dictates of right reason. If a modern reader, chastened by the findings of comparative anthropology, begins to suspect that Price was a victim of urbane parochialism, confirmation is not far to seek. For at the end of his argument, Price gives away the secret of all the assumptions on which his discussion of morals is built—the standard assumptions of a rational, Christian, eighteenth-century English gentleman:

> But, after all, were every observation of this kind wrong, little regard would be due, in these enquiries, to what takes place

amongst those whom we know to be the corrupt and perverted part of the species. Such, most certainly, cannot be the proper persons by whom to judge of truth, or from whom to take our estimate of human nature.[19]

At last we see that those *"eternal and immutable"* principles of morality, which are not "the *arbitrary production* of any power human or divine," [20] are equivalent to the home truths of the English Enlightenment.

In Emerson we find exactly the solution noted in Price's *Review* to the problem of finding universal justification for the dictates of the inner voice. Like Price, Emerson sees in his own habits and arguments an infallible paradigm for all mankind, thereby unwittingly demonstrating how, in morals, Emersonian self-reliance innocently shades off into self-apotheosis. And despite Yvor Winters' denunciation of Emerson as a "moral relativist" and the father of ethical chaos in American thought,[21] the careful student of Emerson's writings finds that the opposite is true: Emerson is much closer to being an absolutist in morals. The trouble is that Emerson often *seems* to be a relativist without actually being one.

In order to document his point, Professor Winters quotes the following well-known lines from "Self-Reliance":

> Whoso would be a man, must be a nonconformist. He who would gather immortal palms must not be hindered by the name of goodness, but must explore if it be goodness. Nothing is at last sacred but the integrity of your own mind. Absolve you to yourself, and you shall have the suffrage of the world. I remember an answer which when quite young I was prompted to make to a valued adviser who was wont to importune me with the dear old doctrines of the church. On my saying, "What have I to do with the sacredness of traditions, if I live wholly from within?" my friend suggested,—"But these impulses may be from below, not from above." I replied, "They do not seem to me to be such; but if I am the Devil's child, I

will live then from the Devil." No law can be sacred to me but that of my nature. Good and bad are but names very readily transferable to that or this; the only right is what is after my constitution; the only wrong what is against it. (C, II, 50) Considered by themselves the lines suggest frightening possibilities; and it may well be, as Professor Winters argues, that taken literally (as he assumes Hart Crane took them) they lead inevitably to moral chaos. But one should read on in Emerson's essay: "The populace think that your rejection of popular standards is a rejection of all standard, and mere antinomianism; and the bold sensualist will use the name of philosophy to gild his crimes. But the law of consciousness abides" (Ibid., 74). Of course, we know what that law is—the moral law. And Emerson finishes his essay by joining the personal and the absolute: "Nothing can bring you peace but yourself. Nothing can bring you peace but the triumph of principles" (Ibid., 90). "Self-Reliance" ends by being simply a higher affirmation of law and order, for the "popular standards" and the standards of Concord were hardly antipodal.

The truth is that Emerson was emphatically not the devil's child. Like the little old Catholic lady in Franklin's *Autobiography* who, living a life of total retirement and purity, still felt the need of a confessor every day, Emerson may have had "vain thoughts"; but he knew well enough he would keep them from passing into violent actions, since "the law of consciousness abides." On January 20, 1832, in a mood seemingly opposed to that of the devil passage from "Self-Reliance," Emerson wrote in his journal: "What a hell should we make of the world if we could do what we would!" (J, II, 450). The contradiction is only apparent. Emerson found it safe and perhaps useful to allow the *awareness* and *articulation* of devilish impulse, since his primary assumption was always the necessity of self-control.

Actually, in spite of what is suggested by the crying up of self-reliance, instinct, and whim, Emerson was basically extremely conservative in morals—not simply in his habits but also in his writings. The young Emerson wrote in his journal in 1823 a passage that might have been composed by Charles Chauncy, the eighteenth-century American rationalist who steadily opposed Jonathan Edwards and the revivalistic Great Awakening:

> Enthusiasm is . . . apt to generate in uncultivated minds a rash and ignorant contempt for the slow modes of education and the cautious arts of reasoning by which enlightened men arrive at wisdom. . . . The boor becomes philosopher at once, and boldly issues the dogmas of a religious creed from the exuberance of a coarse imagination. The tumults of a troubled mind are mistaken for the inspiration of an apostle, and the strength of excited feelings is substituted for the dispassionate and tardy induction, the comparison of scripture and reason, which sanctions the devotions of moderate and liberal men.
> (J, I, 212)

This is early Emerson. Later the vocabulary will change—"reason" will be capitalized and take on new meaning, and "scripture" will tend to drop out—but the attitude will remain the same. Does Emerson contradict the passage quoted above when he writes in "Circles" that "nothing great was ever achieved without enthusiasm. The way of life is wonderful; it is by abandonment" (C, II, 321–22)? Hardly, for we have learned earlier in the essay that the "abandonment" condoned here is abandonment to God and the moral law. And the characteristic Emersonian distrust of enthusiasm reappears in "Culture": "Beware of the man who says, 'I am on the eve of a revelation' " (C, VI, 133).

It is all a question, finally, of what is revealed. A man's individuality or "bias"—"in morals this is conscience" (C,

VIII, 307)—is a fit guide for conduct when it agrees with the
consensus gentium. Self-reliance is not egotistical or dangerous
when the self is virtuous:

> Ignorant people confound reverence for the intuitions with
> egotism. There is no confusion in the things themselves. The
> health of the mind consists in the perception of law. Its
> dignity consists in being under the law. Its goodness is the
> most generous extension of our private interests to the dignity
> and generosity of ideas. Nothing seems to me so excellent as a
> belief in the laws. It communicates nobleness, and, as it were,
> an asylum in temples to the loyal soul. (*Ibid.,* 342)

The key phrase here is, of course, "ignorant people." There is
no confusion in morals when we are among equals and friends.
Emerson, in this respect, sometimes sounds like a model
eighteenth-century English gentleman, such as Lord
Chesterfield—whom, in fact, he quotes approvingly (*Ibid.,*
87).

In "Social Aims," Emerson asserts the corollary: "Self-
control is the rule. You have in you there a noisy, sensual
savage, which you are to keep down, and turn all his strength
to beauty" (*Ibid.*). And again, in "Character": "It were an
unspeakable calamity if any one should think he had the right
to impose a private will on others. That is the part of a striker,
an assassin. All violence, all that is dreary and repels, is not
power but the absence of power" (*C,* X, 92). Of course man
has freedom of the will: how else should he be modern and
liberal? "But will, pure and perceiving, is not wilfulness.
When a man, through stubbornness, insists to do this or that,
something absurd or whimsical, only because he will, he is
weak" (*Ibid.*). We are free only to do that which is good, just,
and honest (as John Winthrop had said in 1645, when he
defined civil liberty [22]); and our arbiter will be Emerson, who
insists that "the high, contemplative, all-commanding vision,
the sense of Right and Wrong, is alike in all" (*C,* X, 93).

Emerson, then, like Price and many other eighteenth-century English writers, conceived it "an advance" that "the mind of [his] age [had] fallen away from theology to morals" (*Ibid.,* 108). He attacked institutionalized religion for worshipping topical "goblins" and advised those of his readers who were tired of "forms" and hungry for something new to worship the one true god, the moral sentiment:

> Every particular instruction is speedily embodied in a ritual, is accommodated to humble and gross minds, and corrupted. The moral sentiment is the perpetual critic on these forms, thundering its protest, sometimes in earnest and lofty rebuke; but sometimes also it is the source, in natures less pure, of sneers and flippant jokes of common people, who feel that the forms and dogmas are not true for them, though they do not see where the error lies. (*Ibid.,* 104)

The error lies, of course, in discarding the faith along with the worn-out forms. Even though the forms and dogmas of Christianity may be untenable, we are not justified in ceasing to remain Christians at heart. Emerson's doctrine of the sovereignty of private inspiration circles safely back on itself. Transcendentalism was indeed a "Saturnalia or excess of faith" (*C,* I, 338), but for Emerson the faith was a belief in traditional ethical standards, and the excess was never convulsive.

As we have noted, this phenomenon in Emerson's thought has parallels in the eighteenth century. Locke, as Sir Leslie Stephen points out, shrewdly used the example of the man-eating "Tououpinambos" to refute innate ideas and smug parochialism and then observed satirically that

> "the principles which all men allow for true are innate; those that men of right reason admit are the principles allowed by all mankind; we, and those of our mind, are men of reason; wherefore, we agreeing, our principles are innate—which is a very pretty way of arguing and a short cut to infallibility." The real fact is, that men, having taken up many principles on

trust, and having entirely forgotten whence they came, assume them to be divinely implanted axioms; and thus "doctrines that have been derived from no better original than the superstition of a nurse and the authority of an old woman may, by length of time and consent of neighbours, grow up to the dignity of principles in morality and religion." [23]

Nevertheless, for all his skepticism, Locke remained a Christian—much more so than Emerson, since he apparently believed in revelation and the divinity of Christ. Although Locke had shown that morality, philosophically considered, is a relative affair, he had no desire to conclude from this that any decent Englishman was free to act in an unchristian way. So, too, with Emerson. The inner oracle is to be the new fountain of truth, in place of the uninspired dictates of the unregenerate understanding; yet if the heart teaches what the head has always agreed to, where is the dispute? Inspiration is admissible, but not when it inspires anything that is "dreary and repels." If Locke regarded Christianity, as Stephen tells us, "less as the revelation of the true relations of man to his Maker than as a new promulgation of the moral law," [24] how did he differ from Emerson, who reduced the religious experience to a reaffirmation of Christian ethics and enshrined the golden rule in the seat of the most high? As Emerson wrote in his essay "Character": "The moral sentiment is alone omnipotent" (C, X, 96).

The point is that Locke would have considered himself no more responsible for the radical conclusions which, according to Victor Cousin,[25] were drawn from the implications of his philosophy by eighteenth-century Continental apologists for atheism and revolution than Emerson would have considered himself accountable for the excesses of Hart Crane and Henry Miller. Nor did Emerson attack Locke (any more than he would have reproached himself) for having spawned a theory of moral relativity. What he disliked in Locke was mainly that philosopher's excess of reason and lack of poetry.[26] Emerson was angry at Locke for denying that one could intuit absolute truth, but they had no quarrel when it came to the nature of that truth. Like Locke himself, Emerson drew back from the potentially dangerous implications of Locke's philosophy (as he did, very quickly, from the wildly idealistic implications of his own *Nature*) and simply argued about method. Jonathan Edwards had come to terms with Locke much more boldly a full century before.

Emerson, however, went on assailing Locke's epistemology. In 1865 he copied into his journal a sentiment of Sampson Reed's that he had heard some forty-four years earlier at his Harvard commencement: " 'The mind of Locke will not always be the measure of Human Understanding' " (*J*, X, 95). Stuck firmly, as it were, at his starting point, Emerson continued attacking the man who had given modern philosophy its major impetus, offering in place of Locke's psychology nothing but the unproved and unprovable assertion, found long before in Dr. Price's *Review*, that the mind has a faculty which intuits absolute truth.[27] Of the possibility of a religious experience having nothing to do with intimations of morality Emerson seemed unaware, or perhaps even frightened. He wrote in his journal in 1823: "There is danger of a *poetical* religion from the tendencies of the age" (*J*, I, 297).

II

In the late 1880's, James Freeman Clarke, always a staunch Transcendentalist, set down in his *Autobiography* the history of his transformation, in the early 1830's, to the new creed:

> The books of Locke, Priestly, Hartley, and Belsham were in my grandfather Freeman's library, and the polemic of Locke against innate ideas was one of my earliest philosophical lessons. But something within me revolted at all such attempts to explain soul out of sense, deducing mind from matter, or

tracing the origin of ideas to nerves, vibrations, and vibra-
tiuncles. So I concluded I had no taste for metaphysics and
gave it up, until Coleridge showed me from Kant that though
knowledge begins *with* experience it does not come *from*
experience. Then I discovered that I was born a Transcendentalist . . .[28]

A good deal of American intellectual history is summarized in
this passage. It shows how several generations of American
thinkers—Emerson among them—were able to pass through
an upsetting storm of contemporary philosophy unscathed and
end up very close to where they began. Certainly a majority of
the Transcendentalists were "born" with their assumptions,
largely imbibed from eighteenth-century British ethical philosophers. And as they had no need of being convinced about
what they believed, so they were unaffected by the skeptical
implications of the new philosophy; they simply searched for
and found what they wanted. As William Ellery Channing's
nephew said of his uncle: "In Kant's doctrine of the Reason
he found confirmation of the views which, in early years
received from Price, had quickened him to ever deeper reverence of the essential powers of man." [29] Ultimately Kant was
expendable, since all that was necessary for salvation could be
found in Price.

    Emerson very nearly burst into song over the "new
thought" in an excited letter to his brother Edward. In the late
1820's and early 1830's he had been reading Coleridge, especially James Marsh's edition of *Aids to Reflection,* and on May
31, 1834, he breathlessly announced his discovery of
idealism—both epistemological and ontological—and of the
new distinction between "Reason" and "Understanding":

    Philosophy affirms that the outward world is only phenomenal
    & the whole concern of dinners of tailors of gigs of balls
    whereof men make such account is a quite relative & tempo-
    rary one—an intricate dream—the exhalation of the present

state of the soul—wherein the Understanding works incessantly as if it were real but the eternal Reason when now &
then he is allowed to speak declares it is an accident a smoke
nowise related to his permanent attributes. Now that I have
used the words, let me ask you do you draw the distinction of
Milton Coleridge & the Germans between Reason & Understanding. I think it a philosophy itself. & like all truth very
practical. . . . Reason is the highest faculty of the soul—what
we mean often by the soul itself; it never *reasons,* never
proves, it simply perceives; it is vision. The Understanding
toils all the time, compares, contrives, adds, argues, near
sighted but strong-sighted, dwelling in the present the expe-
dient the customary. Beasts have some understanding but no
Reason. Reason is potentially perfect in every man—Understanding in very different degrees of strength. The thoughts of
youth, & 'first thoughts,' are the revelations of Reason. the love
of the beautiful & of Goodness as the highest beauty the belief
in the absolute & universal superiority of the Right & the
True . . .[30]

That Kant had denied ontological idealism was probably unknown to Emerson, as was the fact that by "Pure Reason" Kant
really meant "Pure Understanding," denying to Emerson's
"Reason" an objective state of existence. What was important
at the moment was simply Coleridge's statement in *Aids to
Reflection* that "Reason is the Power of universal and necessary
convictions, the Source and Substance of Truths above sense,
and having their evidence in themselves." [31] Here was Price's
"understanding," or intuition, in a new dress; and Emerson
accepted Coleridge's vocabulary eagerly.[32]

Coleridge himself went to Kant, and the Germans in
general, for the same reason that Emerson did: to find philosophical justification for what had originally been Christian
beliefs. Perhaps Coleridge got more than he wanted; for
according to Arthur Lovejoy, he ultimately found in the
Kantian distinction between the "noumenal" and the "phenom-

enal" ego an esoteric denial of freedom of the will and a vindication of original sin.[33] But this is something about which Emerson, so far as one can tell, knew nothing. For him, as for Coleridge, the major thing that Kant seemed to justify was the claim that the "Reason" intuits absolute truth. Coleridge's important misreading of Kant in this respect has been well outlined by C. E. Vaughan:

> . . . by his use of the distinction between the "reason" and the "understanding"—a distinction originally due to Kant—for the purpose of bolstering up opinions originally derived from a wholly different source, he [Coleridge] opens the door to all kinds of fallacies and perversions. With Kant, the distinction between the reason and the understanding has a purely restrictive purpose. Its effect is to deny to the former anything more than a "regulative" or suggestive function in the ordering of knowledge; and to claim from the latter, which, from its nature, must always go hand in hand with a sensible intuition, the sole title to the discovery of truth.[34]

The important thing to note is that Coleridge, by claiming for "speculative Reason" (Pure Reason) the field of what he called *"formal* (or abstract) truth," opened the way to a mixing of "Pure" and "Practical" Reason.[35] Coleridge confused the two by using the word "truth" in connection with Pure Reason, which in Kant has only to do with the forms and categories of human perception, not with moral truth.

Of course, Coleridge is not entirely to blame. Jacobi and Schelling, among others, also found a strain of thought in Kant which seemed to justify Transcendentalism, and as Arthur Lovejoy has carefully demonstrated, Kant is partially at fault for this.[36] In the main, however, Kant is extremely skeptical of any claims that the mind has the power of intuiting absolute truth. Indeed, Lovejoy calls attention to an article of Kant's, written to refute Jacobi, which makes Kant's attitude toward Transcendentalism quite clear:

. . . a so-called philosophy is now advertised in which, in order to possess all philosophical wisdom, one has no need to work, but has only to listen to and enjoy the oracle that speaks within oneself. It is announced that those who follow this philosophy . . . are able by a single penetrating glance into their own inwards to accomplish all that others can achieve by the utmost industry—and, indeed, much more . . . it is only the philosopher of intuition who can assume this *genteel* air, since he alone discovers his own nature, not by the herculean labor of self-knowledge built up patiently from the foundations, but by a sort of self-apotheosis which enables him to soar above all this vulgar task-work. When he speaks, it is upon his own authority; and there is no one who is entitled to call him to account. . . .

The pretension to philosophize under the influence of a higher *feeling* is best of all adapted to produce this genteel tone. For who will deny that I *have* the feeling? And if I can make people believe that this feeling is not merely a subjective peculiarity of my own, but can be possessed by everybody, and that consequently it is something objective, a genuine piece of knowledge attained, not by reasoning from concepts, but by an intuition which grasps the object itself—then I enjoy a great advantage over all those who must first justify their statements before they are entitled to regard them as true. . . . So hurrah for the philosophy of feeling, which leads us directly to the reality itself! [37]

Kant might almost have been writing an attack on Emerson. Moreover, Kant's views and tone here present a strikingly ironic contrast to the portrait of Kant which Emerson gives us in "The Over-Soul":

The great distinction between teachers sacred or literary . . . between philosophers like Spinoza, Kant and Coleridge, and philosophers like Locke, Paley, MacKintosh and Stewart,—between men of the world who are reckoned accomplished talkers, and here and there a fervent mystic, prophesy-

half insane under the infinitude of his thought,—is that one class speaks *from within,* or from experience, as parties and possessors of the fact; and the other class *from without,* as spectators merely, or perhaps as acquainted with the fact on the evidence of third persons. (*C,* II, 287)

The image of Kant (or even Spinoza) as a "fervent mystic prophesying half insane under the infinitude of his thought" would have amused the temperate Königsberg professor. It is also interesting to note that by 1841 Emerson had excommunicated Stewart along with Locke, despite the fact that the former's "moral sense" was still an extremely important element in Emerson's philosophy. Perhaps it was simply because Stewart was associated with the "common sense" school of Scottish philosophy. Names meant a great deal to Emerson, as he himself tells us: ". . . under the names of Heraclitus, Zoroaster, Plato, Kant . . . I get . . . a vocabulary for my ideas. I get no ideas" (*J,* IV, 256). This not only suggests that Emerson was bound philosophically to remain close to what he was at the beginning; it also shows how he came to be known as a Kantian with what are essentially un-Kantian notions.

As René Wellek has pointed out, Emerson's mistake in his description of Kant's philosophy in "The Transcendentalist" was to confuse the "forms" by which the mind experiences with "intuitions of the mind itself." [38] In fact, Emerson, mixing the "transcendent" and the "transcendental," calls the forms a "class of ideas" (*C,* I, 340). Not even Madame de Staël (whose *Germany* Emerson read in 1821) made the mistake of equating space and time with anything innate or intuited; intuitions she relegated to the realm of the heart.[39] But for Emerson the need to dignify the intuitions of the soul with the name "imperative forms" was stronger than his desire really to understand what Kant was saying. What he thought he found in Kant was simply the reinforcement of an old idea of his own. In 1822 he had written in his journal:

> The invisible connection between heaven and earth . . . the
> solitary principle which unites intellectual beings to an
> Account and makes of Men, Moral beings—Religion—is
> . . . distinct and peculiar alike in its origin and in its end
> from all other relations. It is essential to the Universe. You
> seek in vain to contemplate the order of things apart from its
> existence: you can no more banish this than you can separate
> from yourself the notions of Space and Duration. (*Jn, I, 61*)

Here religion is clearly as necessary a form of human experience as space and time. Emerson wrote this approximately one
year after reading in Price's *Review* that space, time, *and* morality are alike eternal and immutable.

However, Emerson was never happy as a trinitarian; space,
time, and religion did not really have equal rank in his
hierarchy. In 1820 he copied into his quotation book, under
the heading "Reasonings *a priori*," an argument of Dr. Samuel
Clarke's, based on a passage in Newton's *Principia*, which
suggested that space and time are simply attributes of God.[40]
This idea finds expression in Emersonian terminology in "Self-
Reliance": "Time and space are but physiological colors which
the eye makes, but the soul is light" (*C, II, 66*). Or, more
clearly, in "The Over-Soul": "Before the revelations of the
soul, Time, Space and Nature shrink away" (*Ibid.,* 273).
The "revelations of the soul," then, seem to be prior to, and
more important than, time and space.

What are these revelations? The mystery is cleared up
further on in the essay: "Let man then learn the revelation of
all nature and all thought to his heart; this, namely; that the
Highest dwells with him; that the sources of nature are in his
own mind, if the sentiment of duty is there" (*Ibid.,* 294).
Man is God *if* he has "the sentiment of duty": this is the important proviso that saves Emerson from moral chaos. Emerson's radical subjectivism reduces itself once again, quite
safely, to a law of positive morality.

That this was Emerson's basic sentiment is clear from other essays. In "Worship" we read: "The law is the basis of the human mind. In us, it is inspiration; out there in Nature we see its fatal strength. We call it the moral sentiment" (C, VI, 221). In "Aristocracy" Emerson urges man to revisit the fountain "of the moral sentiments, the parent fountain from which this goodly Universe flows as a wave" (C, X, 66). The dictates of the religious sentiment have been detached from Kant's Practical Reason and placed in the realm of Pure Reason, where, considered by Emerson equivalent to the laws of the mind, they reign benignly as the supreme principles of a moral universe.

It is fairly clear that this is what Emerson got from Kant: a kind of religious solipsism. In his journal for 1843 Emerson wrote: "Kant, it seems, searched the metaphysics of the Self-reverence which is the favorite position of modern ethics, and demonstrated to the Consciousness that itself alone exists" (J, VI, 482). Kant, of course, had demonstrated nothing of the kind. But what was the danger of saying so, if "Consciousness" was equivalent to duty and the moral law? In such a case, even the traditional concept of God was hardly necessary. So Emerson quoted approvingly in his journal a sentence from Colebrooke's *Essays*: "The internal check is the Supreme Being" (J, VII, 110). Orthodox religionists might be shocked, but where was the harm, since the same old principles were believed in as before?

The harm was, in the first place, that Emerson put too much faith in the innate goodness of man. He himself was gentle and benign, but as Santayana theorized in his discussion of German philosophy:

> . . . a later and more advanced transcendentalist, instead of God, freedom, and immortality, might just as dutifully posit matter, empire, and the beauty of a warrior's death. His conscience might no longer be an echo of Christianity, but the

trumpetblast of a new heathenism. It is for the ego who posits to judge what it should posit.[41]

Emerson's "moral sentiment" was obviously powerless to deal with a world which would include rational human beings choosing to be wilfully unchristian and even inhuman. Perhaps Henry Adams was right in calling Emerson *"naïf."* [42]

But the major problem in the fact that Emerson's experience of God turns out to be no more than the shock of conscience is its spiritual and imaginative inadequacy. John Jay Chapman put it well in his essay on Emerson:

> . . . the Moral Law, by insisting that sheer conscience can slake the thirst that rises in the soul, is convicted of falsehood; and this heartless falsehood is the same falsehood that has been put into the porridge of every Puritan child for six generations.[43]

Such poets as Shelley and Byron set out to "slake the thirst" by fronting experience boldly and forcing something brilliant and glittering from it, for (as Shelley has Demogorgon say in *Prometheus Unbound*) "the deep truth is imageless." Not laws, but life in its fullness, was what they wanted—even if it proved to be meretricious. Their way, however, was not Emerson's. He wisely said that he was born "too soon" for Shelley, whom he found "wholly unaffecting" (J, VI, 114). As for Byron, Emerson found his *Manfred* "ridiculous for its purposeless raving" (J, IV, 251; cf. J, VII, 163). What perhaps really distressed Emerson was that they were exploring the possibilities of experience aesthetically, without the safeguard of traditional ethical assumptions. "The moral anarchy of romanticism," as Howard Mumford Jones puts it,[44] repelled Emerson.

But Emerson's neighbor and protégé, Henry Thoreau, was not afraid of anarchy, perhaps because at heart he was no anarchist. As for the moral law, he knew all about it; he had been to school in it. But as a man he wanted to study something more interesting. "Man finds himself in life," he wrote in 1841, "but with no hint for the conduct of an hour.—Conscience only informs that he must *behave*." [45] Thoreau thought he knew how to behave, but he had yet to find out how to live. So, choosing the "skunk cabbage" of Byron as his nosegay, he set out to sense the world. [46]

CHAPTER FIVE

Thoreau's Quarrel
with the Transcendentalists

I

IF ever Henry Thoreau found a friend, a reader of his correspondence is likely to suspect that it was that genial Englishman, Thomas Cholmondeley. Certainly no other token of a genuine love for Thoreau merits comparison with the magnificent gift of forty-four books of Indian philosophy and poetry that Cholmondeley shipped to Thoreau in 1855. Thoreau's response was gleeful; it glows with a warmth of fellow feeling rarely found in such a record as we have of his guarded emotional life.

In the fullest letter extant from Cholmondeley to Thoreau, one can easily spot the attitudes and habits of expression that made him so very clearly Thoreau's kind of man:

> As for me, my life still continues (through the friendship of an unseen hand) a fountain of never-ending delight, a romance renewed every morning, and never smaller to-day than it was yesterday, but always enhancing itself with every breath I draw. I delight myself, I love to live, and if I have been "run down" I am not aware of it.
>
> I often say to God, "What, O Lord, will you do with me in particular? Is it politics, or philosophical leisure, or war, or hunting, or what?" He always seems to answer, "Enjoy your-

self, and leave the rest to itself." . . . It is so great a matter to exist pleasurably. The sensation of Being! [1]

Cholmondeley's candor and zest for life are strikingly similar, in both form and substance, to Thoreau's own expressions of his lust for existence. Thoreau had said in a letter to H. G. O. Blake in 1848, "I love to live"; [2] and in another letter to Blake, written in December 1856 (shortly before he received the letter from Cholmondeley quoted above), he reiterated his love: "I am grateful for what I am & have. My thanksgiving is perpetual. It is surprising how contented one can be with nothing definite—only a sense of existance [sic]." [3]

Considering this strong affinity between Cholmondeley and Thoreau, we can perhaps understand why the sympathetic Englishman, with all the English horror of offending, yet had the temerity to offer his American friend some advice—advice which Thoreau must have pondered very carefully:

> And now to come to yourself. I have your two letters by me, and read them over with deep interest. You are not living altogether as I could wish. You ought to have society. A college, a conventual life is for you. You should be the member of some society not yet formed. You want it greatly, and without this you will be liable to moulder away as you get older. *Forgive my English plainness of speech.* Your love for, and intimate acquaintance with, Nature is ancillary to some affection which you have not yet discovered. . . . The lonely man is a diseased man, I greatly fear. See how carefully Mr. Emerson avoids it; and yet, who dwells, in all essentials, more religiously free than he? [4]

In reading this, Thoreau, who certainly believed in his own genius, may have been moved to remind his friend that Aristotle allows that the lonely man may be a god. Moreover, Cholmondeley's love of nature here shows itself to have been somewhat different from Thoreau's passionate appetite for the wild. This is not to say that Thoreau himself never wavered in the direction of Cholmondeley's own conclusions on the subject. In June 1852, when his estrangement from Emerson was undoubtedly weighing on him, Thoreau could write in his journal: "A lover of Nature is pre-eminently a lover of man. If I have no friend, what is Nature to me? She ceases to be morally significant" (W, X, 163). But it was only in a rare mood of personal dejection that he would insist on nature's being *morally* significant. A month later, on July 26, 1852, he had returned to his usual position: "By my intimacy with nature I find myself withdrawn from man. My interest in the sun and the moon, in the morning and the evening, compels me to solitude" (W, X, 258). On the following day the subject was still occupying his mind, and he wrote in a vein which indicates that he considered nature primary, not ancillary, in his affections:

> I am sure that if I call for a companion in my walk I have relinquished in my design some closeness of communion with Nature. The walk will surely be more commonplace. The inclination for society indicates a distance from Nature. I do not design so wild and mysterious a walk. (W, X, 262)

That this was Thoreau's usual attitude, public as well as private, is corroborated by an entry in Emerson's journal for 1850: "Nature, Ellery [Channing] thought, is less interesting. Yesterday Thoreau told me it was more so, and persons less" (J, VIII, 122). Thoreau's position may have been defensive; but, particularly after the fiasco of *A Week,* he needed all the defenses he could muster.

As a matter of fact, Cholmondeley's mention of Emerson in his letter to Thoreau must have struck Thoreau with particular irony. For Thoreau's major attempt to "have society," as Cholmondeley suggested, had been directed toward Emerson and had simply come to nothing. Cholmondeley had noted (clearly suggesting whom Thoreau was to emulate) that Emerson carefully avoids solitude, "and yet, who dwells, in all essentials, more religiously free than he?" One suspects that Thoreau had a rather immodest answer for that question. At any rate, Thoreau had anticipated Cholmondeley's suggestion five years earlier, in a journal entry for October 10, 1851, at the time of his crisis with Emerson. It reveals more than anything else why Thoreau failed to find in Emerson the spiritual companion he sought:

> Ah, I yearn toward thee, my friend, but I have not confidence in thee. We do not believe in the same God. . . . Why are we related, yet thus unsatisfactorily? We almost are a sore to one another. Ah, I am afraid because thy relations are not my relations. Because I have experienced that in some respects we are strange to one another, strange as some wild creature. Ever and anon there will come the consciousness to mar our love that, change the theme but a hair's breadth, and we are tragically strange to one another. . . . when I consider what my friend's relations and acquaintances are, what his tastes and habits, then the difference between us gets named. I see that all these friends and acquaintances and tastes and habits are indeed my friend's self. In the first place, my friend is prouder than I am,—and I am very proud, perchance. (W, IX, 61–62)

To begin on the level of "tastes and habits," it is clear that Emerson's fastidiousness, which was taken by others to be a measure of spiritual elevation, galled and alienated Thoreau. "A man," he wrote in 1853, "can't ask properly for a piece of bread and butter without some animal spirits. A child can't cry without them" (W, XI, 43). Was friendship possible without them? Emerson, by his own admission, completely lacked "animal spirits." How, then, could Thoreau—who above all wanted to get a *bite* on his friends—express his cantankerous love for Emerson, who pleaded detachment and offered a philosophical stone when Thoreau wanted the bitter crust of opposition to gnaw on? Certainly a hearty Englishman such as

Cholmondeley would have understood Thoreau's difficulty. Emerson himself, in his *English Traits*, had praised the English for their pluck:

> They dare to displease, they do not speak to expectation. They like the sayers of No, better than the sayers of Yes. Each of them has an opinion which he feels it becomes him to express all the more that it differs from yours. They are meditating opposition. This gravity is inseparable from minds of great resources. (*C*, V, 136)

Emerson's description also fits Thoreau very well, though Thoreau could often appear to be acting contrary to Emerson simply for contrariness' sake, as in this journal entry for 1852: "R. W. E. tells me he does not like Haynes as well as I do. I tell him that he makes better manure than most men" (*W*, X, 15). Nevertheless, there does seem to be a point to Henry's gibe: couldn't Emerson take men as they came and thus get the good out of them? Worse yet, it seems clear that Emerson was suggesting that Thoreau's taste in friends was low. If so, Thoreau got back at his noble friend in 1858, when he recorded one of his liveliest journal entries on Emerson:

> Emerson says that he and Agassiz and Company broke some dozens of ale-bottles, one after another, with their bullets, in the Adirondack country, using them for marks! It sounds rather Cockneyish. He says that he shot a peetweet for Agassiz, and this, I think he said, was the first game he ever bagged. He carried a double-barrelled gun,—rifle and shotgun,—which he bought for the purpose, which he says received much commendation,—all parties thought it a very pretty piece. Think of Emerson shooting a peetweet (with shot) for Agassiz, and cracking an ale-bottle (after emptying it) with his rifle at six rods! They cut several pounds of lead out of the tree. It is just what Mike Saunders, the merchant's clerk, did when he was there. (*W*, XVII, 119–120)

In reading such a passage, the student of Emerson and Thoreau must find himself drawn in different directions. Insofar as
the expedition (and the relation of it) represented the attempt
of Emerson, the withdrawn intellectual, to be "regular," to
participate in what he must have considered the necessary
mundane pastimes of good fellows on an outing, one can only
sympathize. But from Thoreau's side, what business had Emerson complaining of his friendship with Haynes if Emerson and
Agassiz behaved no better than Mike Saunders? Well-made
manure, Thoreau might have argued, is better than broken ale
bottles. Although one might justly accuse Thoreau of being
somewhat stiff-necked in his judgment of a harmless episode,
the point still remains that Emerson's pride in the sublimity of
his own opinions and manners must have struck Thoreau as
excessive, if not positively unwarranted.

Indeed, it was Emerson's pride, particularly in his ideas,
that undoubtedly irritated Thoreau most. It led to conde-
scension and an assumption of discipleship which Thoreau was
never prepared to accept. All of literary New England knew
that Thoreau was not much more than a sharp-tongued follower of Emerson. And no one knew it better than Emerson
himself, who in 1841 recorded the following in his journal:

> I told Henry Thoreau that his freedom is in the form, but he
> does not disclose new matter. I am very familiar with all his
> thoughts,—they are my own quite originally drest. But if the
> question be, what new ideas has he thrown into circulation, he
> has not yet told what that is which he was created to say. (J,
> VI, 74)

As a matter of fact, as far as Emerson was concerned, Thoreau
never did tell what, in any truly original sense, he might have
been created to say. For although in "Historic Notes of Life
and Letters in New England" Emerson credited Thoreau with
having given "in flesh and blood and pertinacious Saxon belief

the purest ethics" (C, X, 356), we may note how much there is of self-congratulation in Emerson's praise by comparing it with the original statement as it appears in Emerson's journal for 1852: "Thoreau gives me, in flesh and blood and pertinacious Saxon belief, my own ethics" (J, VIII, 303). The purity of Thoreau's ethics, Emerson seems to have felt, could only have been Emersonian.

This Thoreau was not prepared to admit, as we may note by recalling his journal passage on Emerson: "Ah, I yearn toward thee, my friend, but I have not confidence in thee. We do not believe in the same God. . . . change the theme but a hair's breadth, and we are tragically strange to one another." This is simply the expression, which here became overt at the time of Thoreau's personal crisis with Emerson, of something that Thoreau had known for a long time: somebody in Concord was worshipping strange gods. Indeed, the difference between Emerson and Thoreau had gotten named as early as 1836, when Emerson made the following entry in his journal:

> The reality which the ancient mind attributed to all things, equally to the fictions of the poets and to the facts observed by their own eyes, is most remarkable. . . . They seem to be no transcendentalists,—to rest always in the spontaneous consciousness. (J, IV, 141–142)

Emerson furnishes us here with a fair summary of what was to be Thoreau's basic position. Who, then, was the Transcendentalist? And why could not the Concord School become the "college" or "conventual life" that Cholmondeley so earnestly wished for Thoreau?

II

On July 13, 1852, Thoreau wrote a letter to his sister Sophia which includes a rather different description of Concord from what we are accustomed to associate with the home

of Emerson, Thoreau, and Hawthorne. Apparently there was a
kind of second-rate Transcendentalism being practiced in respectable front parlors:

> Concord is just as idiotic as ever in relation to the spirits and
> their knockings. Most people here believe in a spiritual world
> which no respectable junk bottle which had not met with a
> slip—would condescend to contain even a portion of for a
> moment. . . . Where *are* the heathen? Was there ever any
> superstition before? And yet I suppose there may be a vessel
> this very moment setting sail from the coast of North America
> to that of Africa with a missionary on board! Consider the
> dawn & the sun rise—the rain bow & the evening,—the words
> of Christ & the aspirations of all the saints! Hear music?
> See—smell—taste—feel—hear—anything—& then hear these
> idiots inspired by the cracking of a restless board—humbly
> asking "Please spirit, if you cannot answer by knocks, answer
> by tips of the table."!!!!!! [5]

It is tantalizing to wonder just who was experimenting with
this nineteenth-century version of the Ouija board, but we can
be satisfied with the point of Thoreau's letter—the same point
that led to his stridently anti-religious outburst in the "Sunday"
section of *A Week*. It distressed him to note that for many of
his neighbors, the life of the spirit amounted to little more than
superstition, and he repeated the complaint in his journal for
1853:

> . . . we have only to be reminded of the kind of respect paid
> to the Sabbath as a *holy* day here in New England, and the
> fears which haunt those who *break* it, to see that our neighbors
> are the creatures of an equally gross superstition with the
> ancients. . . . The New-Englander is a pagan suckled in a
> creed outworn. Superstition has always reigned. (*W*, XI, 223)

So much for the common people of Concord. As for Thoreau,
we may mark in passing the particularly Thoreauvian note, at

the end of his letter, in which religious vision and experience are linked through the careful enumeration of the five senses—Thoreau's only Ouija board.

Even granting, however, that what passed for spirituality among the ordinary townspeople was offensive to Thoreau, one might at least suggest that he had the exhilarating new thought of his authentically Transcendental brethren with which to associate himself. Certainly there was no patience among them for superstition or worn-out forms; they devoted themselves to elevated talk of the infinite, of non-historical revelation, and of the divine within every man. What then, Cholmondeley might have asked, was Thoreau's excuse for his dogged solitude, for his tragically holding himself aloof from the only true friends New England offered him? There was perhaps no excuse—except Thoreau's clear aversion, apparent early and late in his writings, to most of what we have come to associate with Transcendentalism.

Thoreau expressed his plight in a journal poem entitled "The Fisher's Son" (1840), several stanzas of which are particularly relevant.[6] In the first stanza, he reveals his station and method in life:

> I know the world where land and water meet,
> By yonder hill abutting on the main;
> One while I hear the waves incessant beat,
> Then, turning round, survey the land again.
> (*W*, VII, 110)

Thoreau's peculiar spot in life is the point of contact between "land and water," between the eternal and temporal realms. His job is to keep in touch with both spirit and matter. This position, however, puts him in an unfortunate relation to those around him, as several more stanzas of the poem indicate:

I have no fellow-laborer on the shore;
They scorn the strand who sail upon the sea;
Sometimes I think the ocean they've sailed o'er
Is deeper known upon the strand to me.

The middle sea can show no crimson dulse,
Its deeper waves cast up no pearls to view,
Along the shore my hand is on its pulse,
Whose feeble beat is elsewhere felt by few.

My neighbors come sometimes with lumb'ring carts,
As it would seem my pleasant toil to share,
But straightway take their loads to distant marts,
For only weeds and ballast are their care.
        (*Ibid.*, 111–12)

Perhaps it did seem occasionally to Thoreau that such worthy
Concord neighbors as the farmers Goodwin, Haynes, and
Minott were his most fit companions. But ultimately, despite
the refreshing sanity of their concrete notions, Thoreau would
come to feel that their real concern was with "weeds and
ballast." As for the more ethereal Concordians, those who spent
much of their time sailing on the ocean of infinity, their
"scorn" of "the strand" was to be the source of some humor
and of a great deal of tension between them and Thoreau.
What were those Don Quixotes to do with this starry-eyed
Sancho Panza, who insisted on measuring the depth of Walden Pond because he thought it "remarkable how long men
will believe in the bottomlessness of a pond without taking the
trouble to sound it"—only to conclude, rather oddly: "While
men believe in the infinite some ponds will be thought to be
bottomless" (*W*, II, 315–16)?

"Modern philosophy," Thoreau noted in 1840, "thinks it
has drawn down lightning from the clouds" (*W*, VII, 125).
Undoubtedly he considered a good deal of the "new thought"

to be more like thunder: sometimes simply ingenuous rumblings on the eternal, but at other times the fanfaronade of vaguely hypocritical pomposity. As he noted in 1854: "I meet with several who cannot afford to be simple and true men, but personate, so to speak, their own ideal of themselves, trying to make the manners supply the place of the man. They are puffballs filled with dust and ashes" (*W*, XII, 200).

The history of many of Thoreau's Transcendental friendships is the sadly predictable tale of the painful disparity between the real men he tried to befriend and the ideal they offered him instead. Perhaps the most characteristic and interesting friendship in this respect was that between Thoreau and William Ellery Channing, the poetic nephew of the great Unitarian leader. Channing was Thoreau's most constant companion, and there was undoubtedly a good deal of affection between them; but Thoreau's journal passages on Channing, when not downright condemnatory, are tinged with a gentle irony which signals his awareness of Channing's Transcendental blind spots. In the first place, since a return to nature was supposed to be the keystone of the new philosophy, Channing was by definition a nature lover, but his methods distressed Thoreau:

> In our walks C. takes out his note-book sometimes and tries to write as I do, but all in vain. He soon puts it up again, or contents himself with scrawling some sketch of the landscape. Observing me still scribbling, he will say that he confines himself to the ideal, purely ideal remarks; he leaves the facts to me. Sometimes, too, he will say a little petulantly, "I am universal; I have nothing to do with the particular and definite." (*W*, IX, 98–99)

If Channing was trying to rationalize his indifference to natural phenomena by suggesting that Thoreau, like Dr. Bat in Cooper's *The Prairie*, was a vile empiric devoid of the higher sense, the inference clearly riled Thoreau, who carried the argument into his journal. His facts, he insisted, were "not facts to assist men to make money, farmers to farm profitably, in any common sense. . . . My facts shall be falsehoods to the common sense. I would so state facts that they shall be significant, shall be myths or mythologic" (*Ibid.*, 99). Nevertheless, facts they were. And Thoreau believed that he who would "have nothing to do with the particular and definite" could scarcely hope to reach the "ideal"—whatever that might turn out to be. Three days later Thoreau concluded quite simply that Channing would fail: "C. is one who will not stoop to rise. . . . He wants something for which he will not pay the going price" (*Ibid.*, 108). The price was thorough immersion in experience, but Channing's notion of experience was evidently different from Thoreau's, as the latter indicated in another journal passage on his metaphysically minded friend: "Channing showed me last night on a map where, as he said, he 'used to walk' in Rome. He was there sixteen days" (*W*, XII, 61–62). To Thoreau, whose passion for walking amounted almost to religious mania, sixteen days was a ludicrously short time in which to get the usable facts of a place into one's bones.

What perhaps really bothered Thoreau about Channing's ideals, however, was that they often seemed curiously at variance with his habits. "When I was at C.'s the other evening," he recorded in his journal for 1854, "he punched his cat with the poker because she purred too loud for him" (*Ibid.*, 75). For Channing a profession of Transcendental idealism was apparently not inconsistent with a lack of reverence for the lower forms of life. Indeed, we might include the lower ranks of society:

> Two young men who borrowed my boat the other day returned from the riverside through Channing's yard, quietly. It was almost the only way for them. But, as they passed out

his gate, C. boorishly walked out his house behind them in his shirt-sleeves, and shut his gate again behind them as if to shut them out. It was just that sort of behavior which, if he had met with it in Italy or France, he would have complained of, whose meanness he would have condemned. (*W*, XI, 189–90)

Thoreau, it seems, was intimating that Channing was only Transcendental north-north-west: when the wind was in the direction of his interests, he could tell an ordinary vagrant from Bronson Alcott. Indeed, Thoreau's experiences with Channing made him realize that his friend's canniness about practical matters rarely slept, as in the anecdote Thoreau relates of the time he and Channing got caught in a pouring rain:

> By this time of course we were wet quite through and through, and C. began to inquire and jest about the condition of our money—a singular prudence methought—and buried his wallet in his pocket-handkerchief and returned it to his pocket again. He thought that bank-bills would be spoiled. It had never occurred to me if a man got completely wet through how it might affect the bank-bills in his wallet, it is so rare a thing for me to have any there. (*Ibid.*, 494)

What saves Thoreau from pharisaical immodesty is, of course, the final clause: the point of the story was less Channing's "singular prudence" than his own habitual poverty.

On his side, Channing was obviously convinced that the lack of perfect understanding between them was owing to Thoreau's naive optimism—the lack of any tragic experience in Thoreau's life. As early as 1845, Channing made this clear in a letter to Thoreau:

> I saw Teufelsdrock a few days since; he is wretchedly poor, has an attack of the colic, & expects to get better immediately. He said a few words to me, about you. Says he, that fellow Thoreau might be something if he would only take a journey through the "Everlasting No," thence for the North Pole. By God," said the old clothes-bag "warming-up," I should like to

take that fellow out into the Everlasting No, & explode him like a bomb-shell; he would make a loud report. He needs the Blumine flower business [i.e., to fall in love]; that would be his salvation. He is too dry, too confused, too chalky, too concrete. I want to get him into my fingers. It would be fun to see him pick himself up." [7]

If, as some of the evidence seems to indicate, Thoreau had proposed to and been rejected by Ellen Sewall in 1840, he had indeed been exploded by the "Blumine flower business." Channing would probably have known nothing of that. But quite apart from a possible abortive romance, the tragic death in 1842 of Thoreau's beloved brother John might conceivably have qualified Thoreau, in Channing's eyes, as a companion in tragedy. Apparently, however, Channing always saw Thoreau as his inferior in depth of experience, as this 1854 journal entry of Thoreau's indicates:

> C.'s skates are not the best, and beside he is far from an easy skater, so that, as he said, it was killing work for him. Time and again the perspiration actually dropped from his forehead on to the ice, and it froze in long icicles on his beard. Yet he kept up his spirits and his fun, said he [had] seen much more suffering than I, etc., etc. (W, XIII, 87)

Here Channing's insistence on tragedy is transformed by Thoreau into high comedy. But it is clear that despite his good-natured journalizing about Channing's pose, Thoreau was distressed by the substitution, certainly in life but especially in Channing's poetry, of high-flown rhetoric for real experience. The absence of felt life, along with the debasing of language, turned both art and life into something not intrinsically serious; and that, for Thoreau, was a serious matter. By way of corrective suggestion, Thoreau thought "it would be a good discipline for Channing, who writes poetry in a sublimo-slipshod style, to write Latin, for then he would be compelled to say something always" (W, IX, 118). But there is no indication that Thoreau's advice ever reached Channing or, if it did, that it helped.

Thoreau's serious criticism of Channing's method and, by extension, of much Transcendental writing in general found its way, somewhat obliquely, into *A Week*. It provides an interesting sidelight on his relation to his Transcendental confreres:

> There are already essays and poems, the growth of this land, which are not in vain, all which, however, we could conveniently have stowed in the till of our chest. . . . Here are they who
>> "ask for that which is our whole life's light,
>> For the perpetual, true, and clear insight."
>
> I remember a few sentences which spring like the sward in its native pasture, where its roots were never disturbed, and not as if spread over a sandy embankment; answering to the poet's prayer,—
>> "Let us set so just
>> A rate on knowledge, that the world may trust
>> The poet's sentence, and not still aver
>> Each art is to itself a flatterer." [8]

The first two lines which Thoreau quotes are Channing's: they are abstract and yearn for an eternal truth outside the terms of the poem and beyond the range of ordinary experience. To answer Channing, Thoreau calls upon the unified sensibility of the English seventeenth century and quotes William Habington. The point to be drawn from his four lines is that poetry must be intrinsically true. What Channing seeks outside his art is illusory, so that his poetry flatters itself: it raises expectations that cannot be satisfied. Thoreau's concern for the typical Transcendental attitude represented by Channing is underlined and extended interestingly in a "poem" of Thoreau's published for the first time by Carl Bode in 1943:

What sought they thus afar
They sought a faith's pure shrine.

Seek! shall I seek! The Gods above should give,
They have enough and we do poorly live.

"I ask today for no external thing,
For sight of upland hill and waving tree,
I do not wish to see the glancing wing
Of bird nor hear with trembling heart her melody,
I ask for that which is our whole life's light,
for the perpetual, true, & clear insight."

Away! away! Thou speakest to me of things which in all my
endless life I have found not and shall not find. . . .

Thy lot, or portion of life, is seeking after thee; therefore be
at rest from seeking after it.[9]

As Carl Bode points out, the quoted section of the "poem" is by
Channing; it is a larger portion of the Channing poem cited by
Thoreau in *A Week*. What Professor Bode failed to note is that
the last two sections of Thoreau's "poem" are also not by
Thoreau: the first ("Away!") is by Jean Paul Richter, the
second ("Thy lot . . .") by the Caliph Ali. Thoreau presumably got them both from Emerson's *Essays* (First Series),
where they appear in "Love" and "Self-Reliance," respectively.
Thoreau simply uses them to refute Channing's position. The
supernal insight which Channing seeks he does not expect to
find through an exploration of the real world. For Channing
nature is fine but external; it does not contain the sublime
answer to the Transcendental question. Thoreau's reply could
only be that an impertinent question is bound to be answerless.
Channing would fail because he was not willing to go deeply
enough into natural experience; his much-vaunted love of
nature was merely superficial.

Indeed, despite a great deal of impassioned talk about nature, Thoreau occasionally received indisputable proof that when it came to a real taste for the wild, he was pretty much alone—and, moreover, suspect on account of his habits. On February 19, 1843, for instance, a "Conversation" was held on just this topic in the Emerson household and was fortunately recorded by Lidian in a letter to her husband (who was lecturing in New York). It gives a clear indication of where Thoreau stood vis-à-vis his Transcendental friends:

> Last evening we had the "Conversation," though, owing to the bad weather, but few attended. The subjects were: What is Prophecy? Who is a Prophet? and The Love of Nature. Mr. Lane decided, as for all time and the race, that this same love of nature—of which Henry was the champion, and Elizabeth Hoar and Lidian (though L. disclaimed possessing it herself) his faithful squiresses—that this love was the most subtle and dangerous of sins; a refined idolatry, much more to be dreaded than gross wickednesses, because the gross sinner would be alarmed by the depth of his degradation, and come up from it in terror, but the unhappy idolaters of Nature were deceived by the refined quality of their sin, and would be the last to enter the kingdom. Henry frankly affirmed to both the wise men that they were wholly deficient in the faculty in question, and therefore could not judge of it. And Mr. Alcott as frankly answered that it was because they went beyond the mere material objects, and were filled with spiritual love and perception (as Mr. T. was not), that they seemed to Mr. Thoreau not to appreciate outward nature.[10]

Lidian thought the scene "ineffably comic," but one suspects that Thoreau was not entirely amused. Cant, even when delivered with utter seriousness, was bound to offend him. Besides, his stake in the question of the importance and value of natural experience was not simply dialectical. Yet he could good-humoredly note in his journal nine years later the same disparity in Alcott between pose and performance that Channing so often exhibited:

> Alcott here the 9th and 10th. He, the spiritual philosopher, is, and has been for some months, devoted to the study of his own genealogy,—he whom only the genealogy of humanity, the descent of man from God, should concern! . . . He who wrote of Human Culture, he who conducted the Conversations on the Gospels, he who discoursed of Sleep, Health, Worship, Friendship, etc., last winter, now reading the wills and the epitaphs of the Alcocks with the zeal of a professed antiquarian and genealogist! (*W*, X, 292–93)

Perhaps this was all the proof Thoreau needed that his belief in the real was more pervasive and serious than Alcott's in the ideal.

Thus it would seem that if Thoreau lacked much conviction about the value of metaphysical speculation, his attitude had more than a little to do with the passionate intensity of the Transcendentalists and their followers, which must have seemed hypocritical, when not absolutely foolish. One wonders, for instance, what Thoreau's reaction was to the letter he received in 1842 from James Richardson, Jr., a Harvard classmate of his:

> I have been desirous of sending to some of my mystic brethren—some selections from certain writings of mine, that wrote themselves, when "I was in the spirit on the Lord's Day." Some of these are so utterly and entirely out of all my rational faculties, that I can't put *any* meaning in them; others I read over, and learn a great deal from. This, I send you, seems to be a sort of Allegory—When you return it, will you be so kind as to tell me all that it means, as there are some parts of it I do not fully understand myself . . .[11]

Unfortunately Thoreau's response, if there was one, is no longer extant. But considering all the mystic literature and specimens of automatic writing that abounded at the time—especially in the early 1840's, when *The Dial* was being published—it is probable that even if Thoreau was inclined to play the part of Richardson's oneirocritic, he already had his hands full. Yet the earnestness of some of the seekers who corresponded with Thoreau could hardly have failed to elicit his sympathy; even if he had no desire to join in their undertakings, he could still admire their spirit. Isaac Hecker, for instance, the New York baker whose passionate pilgrimage finally led him to Rome, must have received at least verbal encouragement from Thoreau during the brief time in the spring of 1844 when he boarded at the Thoreau household, since he was moved, in July of that year, to propose that Thoreau join him in a spiritual exploration of Europe:

> I have been stimulated to write to you at this present moment on account of a certain project which I have formed in which your influence has no slight share I imagine in forming. It is to work our passage to Europe, and to walk, work, and beg, if needs be, as far when there as we are inclined to do. We wish to see how it looks. And to court difficulties, for we feel an unknown depth of untried virgin strength which we know of no better way at the present time to call into activity and so dispose of. We desire to go without purse or staff, depending upon the all embracing love of God, Humanity, and the spark of courage imprisoned in us.[12]

Thoreau's response was cordial, even sympathetic, but contained a typically Thoreauvian rejection of the proposal: he still had much travelling to do in Concord, and "is not here too Roncesvalles with greater lustre?"[13] Nevertheless, Hecker was insistent and repeated his invitation: "The conceivable is possible, it is in harmony with the inconceivable. we should act. Our true life is in the cannot, to do what we can do is to do nothing, is death. Silence is much more respectable than repetition."[14] This time Thoreau's answer was much shorter;

he had already made his point in the previous letter. But it is not impossible that he was put off by Hecker's curious insistence on hardship, deliberately sought out. And certainly Hecker's desire for the "inconceivable" was not in harmony with Thoreau's own views. "The actual," he was to write in 1851, "is fair as a vision or a dream" (W, VIII, 477–78). Not variety, but intensity of experience was what Thoreau wanted, in which case repetition was clearly respectable; indeed, it was necessary. And was it not, after all, just this obsessive concern with the "inconceivable" that constituted the gulf between his fellow Transcendentalists and himself? "James Clark—the Swedenborgian that was," Thoreau wrote to Emerson in 1847, "is at the Poor House—insane with too large views, so that he cannot support himself." [15] The "too large views" were not just comical; they were dangerous when one took them seriously. If cant was the Scylla of Transcendentalism, the Charybdis was possible insanity.

By the mid-1850's, and especially after his break with Emerson, Thoreau seems to have had much less sympathy for the Transcendental desire to voyage in the intense inane. In September 1856, for instance, a Providence businessman named B. B. Wiley initiated a correspondence with him and was soon asking for pronouncements on very high matters: "I am anxious to know a little more of Confucius. Can you briefly, so that it will not take too much of *your* time, write me his views in regard to Creation, Immortality, man's preexistence if he speaks of it, and generally anything relating to man's Origin, Purpose, & Destiny." [16] Thoreau was undoubtedly flattered to be considered an authority on such recondite affairs, but his reply very kindly turned Wiley off:

> I do not now remember anything which Confucius has said directly respecting man's "origin, purpose, and destiny." He was more practical than that. He is full of wisdom applied to human relations—to the private life—the Family—Govern-

ment &c. It is remarkable that according to his own account the sum & substance of his teaching is, as you know, to Do as you would be done by.[17]

Wiley had also asked about Swedenborg, eliciting a somewhat sharper response from Thoreau:

> He comes nearer to answering, or attempting to answer, literally, your questions concerning man's origin, purpose & destiny than any of the worthies I have referred to. But I think that this is not *altogether* a recommendation; since such an answer to these questions cannot be discovered, any more than perpetual motion, for which no reward is now offered.[18]

Thoreau clearly had no desire to offend Wiley. Still, he had undoubtedly by this time heard a sufficient amount of talk of such a nature, and his irony is patent. Long before, in his journal for 1842, he had decided that "man's moral nature is a riddle which only eternity can solve" (*W*, VII, 339). Would Wiley have understood Thoreau's journal entry of 1840: "We *see* truth—we are children of *light*[—]our destiny is *dark*"?[19] The only obscurity, Thoreau implied, lay in the attempt to see things that were simply not visible; the truth was to be found in the actual process of seeing. But it must soon have been obvious to him that what Wiley really wanted he couldn't supply. On December 21, 1856, Wiley wrote:

> Most men here are intensely devoted to trade but I have found one with whom I have unreserved & delightful intercourse— Rev Rush R. Shippen the Unitarian minister. Mr Emerson will remember him. He is no ways priestly but has that open guileless countenance that wins the fullest confidence. He is of course intelligent & well-informed. He generously places his library at my disposal. I gladly accepted an invitation to take tea with him tomorrow as there is entire absence of ceremony. I am glad to find such a man with whom I can talk of the Infinite & Eternal.[20]

Thoreau doubtless read Wiley's description of his Unitarian minister with the same critical and ironic perception that led to James's portrait of Rev. Babcock in *The American* and to Santayana's delicate satire of Rev. Edgar Thornton in *The Last Puritan*. At any rate, Thoreau's final extant letter to Wiley, written in response to Wiley's of December 21st but four months later, is noticeably cool in tone, somewhat cryptic, and decidedly not an invitation to further correspondence. What, after all, had he to say to a man who could discourse of the infinite and eternal with Rev. Rush R. Shippen?

The problem, then, that Thoreau had with most of his friends and correspondents was that their inveterate desire for metaphysical conversation was offensive to him. Moreover, and this was certainly related to the first difficulty, their attitude toward nature was much different from his: they loved it at a distance and homiletically. Only one of Thoreau's friends, H. G. O. Blake, seems to have had any inkling of what he was about and, in his single surviving letter to Thoreau, placed his finger on what separated them:

> I honor you because you abstain from action, and open your soul that you may *be* somewhat. Amid a world of noisy, shallow actors it is noble to stand aside and say, "I will simply *be*." Could I plant myself at once upon the truth, reducing my wants to their minimum, . . . I should at once be brought nearer to nature, nearer to my fellowmen,—and life would be infinitely richer. But, alas! I shiver on the brink . . .[21]

As far as immersion in natural experience was concerned, Thoreau was in alone, leaving his friends to shiver on the brink—some, like Blake, with nostalgic yearning; others, like Channing and Alcott, with a sense of spiritual superiority. "Farewell to those," Thoreau wrote in that crucial summer of 1851, "who will talk of nature unnaturally, whose presence is an interruption" (*W*, VIII, 302). Indeed, Thoreau had complained of this "unnatural" attitude toward nature in even stronger terms in *A Week:*

> The surliness with which the woodchopper speaks of his woods, handling them as indifferently as his axe, is better than the mealy-mouthed enthusiasm of the lover of nature. Better that the primrose by the river's brim be a yellow primrose, and nothing more, than that it be something less." (*W*, I, 111–12)

Quite clearly, Thoreau was here attacking a Correspondential attitude toward nature: to turn the primrose into a symbol was to reduce its value. Did Thoreau, then, not believe in Correspondence? The student finds himself faced with what appears to be a case of Transcendental heresy.

III

In his *American Renaissance,* F. O. Matthiessen writes: "In spite of his keenness in scrutinizing the reports of his senses, Thoreau remained wholly the child of his age in regarding the material world as a symbol of the spiritual." [22] The student of Thoreau who wishes to justify this statement can certainly find material with which to do so, as is probably the case with most writers of the American Renaissance. Hawthorne, for instance, would appear to be a perfect Transcendentalist in "The Old Manse" when he moralizes on the "fragrant white pond-lily" and says of the Concord River: ". . . if we remember its tawny hue and the muddiness of its bed, let it [the fact that the river reflects the heavens] be a symbol that the earthliest human soul has an infinite spiritual capacity and may contain the better world within its depths." [23] Yet, as Matthiessen himself makes abundantly clear, Hawthorne was certainly no believer in Transcendental Correspondence. Perhaps the white water lily is in itself particularly conducive to Transcendentalizing. It seduced Thoreau into one

of his rare patches of baldly Correspondential writing in his
journal for 1854:

> Growing in stagnant and muddy [water], it bursts up so pure
> and fair to the eye and so sweet to the scent, as if to show us
> what purity and sweetness reside in, and can be extracted
> from, the slime and muck of earth. . . . The foul slime
> stands for the sloth and vice of man; the fragrant flower that
> springs from it, for the purity and courage which springs from
> its midst. (W, XII, 352–53)

Thoreau's prose here is flat, as it certainly is also in his longest
exercise in Transcendental writing, sparked by his reading in
Asa Gray—four pages of his 1851 journal devoted to a tedious
attempt at proving that there is "a perfect analogy between the
life of the human being and that of the vegetable, both of the
body and the mind" (W, VIII, 201 ff.). That Thoreau occasionally wrote in such a fashion no one can deny. But what is
striking about Thoreau's writings, taken *in toto,* is the extent to
which he took pains to avoid just the conclusion that Matthiessen draws in *American Renaissance.* Transcendentalism had
another meaning for Thoreau than Emersonian Correspondence.

Thoreau's revolt against this concept, however, is perhaps
all the more surprising when we notice just how clearly he
began his speculative career under the aegis of Emerson. In the
fall of 1839, for instance, he copied into his journal a passage
which reads as if he had been trying to write a précis of
Nature: "We are one virtue, one truth, one beauty. All nature
is our satellite, whose light is dull and reflected. She is subal-
tern to us,—an episode to our poem; but we are primary, and
radiate light and heat to the system" (W, VII, 107). Thirteen
years later—a long time in Thoreau's career—his views had
made a complete about-face:

In order to avoid delusions, I would fain let man go by and behold a universe in which man is but as a grain of sand. . . . I do not value any view of the universe into which man and the institutions of man enter very largely and absorb much of the attention. Man is but the place where I stand, and the prospect hence is infinite. It is not a chamber of mirrors which reflect me. When I reflect, I find that there is other than me. Man is a past phenomenon to philosophy. (*W*, IX, 381–82)

Thoreau's new position was not to involve a forgetting of the self: the shift from a Ptolemaic to a post-Copernican view of the universe may have diminished man's importance, but it enlarged man's interest in his own plight. Thoreau was now simply prepared to announce that the physical universe was intrinsically more important than a reader of Emerson might have been led to believe.

This shift in Thoreau's attitude had become apparent at least as early as 1842. In 1837 he had affirmed: "How indispensable to a correct study of Nature is a perception of her true meaning. The fact will one day flower out into a truth" (*W*, VII, 18). Here certainly is an example of his early training in Correspondence: he is clearly suggesting that a "correct study of Nature" leads to symbolic interpretation. If, as is likely, Emerson knew that these were the sentiments of the young Thoreau, it may have been just such an entry that prompted him to commission "The Natural History of Massachusetts," Thoreau's first important article, for *The Dial* of July 1842.[24] Thoreau, it would seem, could be trusted to open his text in proper Transcendental fashion. But the correction which that 1837 journal entry underwent before it finally appeared in the article points up the subtle change in Thoreau's thinking: "Let us not underrate the value of a fact; it will one day flower in a truth" (*W*, V, 130). Thoreau no longer speaks of the "true meaning" of nature; he simply doubles his insistence on the importance of an accurate perception.

As for the "truth" that will one day emerge, Thoreau does not specify—purposely, it would seem. Emerson undoubtedly thought that the "truth" was moral, perhaps a law of ethics. But Thoreau did not suggest in the article that the best scientist, as Emerson clearly believed, would be a Baconian analogist. He rejected the Baconian method as being "as false as any other" and simply asserted: "The true man of science will know nature better by his finer organization; he will smell, taste, see, hear, feel, better than other men" (*Ibid.*, 131). Characteristically, he insisted only on the precise experience of the senses and left the spiritual laws to fend for themselves. Indeed, a canny reader had every reason to suspect, early in Thoreau's article, that he was not getting an orthodox Emersonian treatment of the subject:

> We fancy that this din of religion, literature, and philosophy, which is heard in pulpits, lyceums, and parlors, vibrates through the universe, and is as catholic a sound as the creaking of the earth's axle; but if a man sleep soundly, he will forget it all between sunset and dawn. It is the three-inch swing of a pendulum in a cupboard, which the great pulse of nature vibrates by and through each instant. When we lift our eyelids and open our ears, it disappears with smoke and rattle like the cars on a railroad. (*Ibid.*, 106)

One wonders whether Emerson's attention had perhaps wandered when he approved this passage for publication, since Thoreau seems here to have been biting the hand that fed him. Emerson had invited Thoreau to write the article because he felt sure that Thoreau would make it clear that the Transcendental—that is, the Correspondential—method applied to nature yields far finer results than the coldly scientific. But what emerges from "The Natural History of Massachusetts" is less an attack on the amassing of scientific data than an expression of disdain for the moralist's insistence on sermons, either in stones or out of them. Thoreau detested moralizing and spiritualizing in literature. His dislike of Ruskin also stemmed from exactly this difficulty:

> After reading Ruskin on the love of Nature, I think, "Drink deep, or taste not the Pierian spring." . . . He has not implicitly surrendered himself to her. And what does he substitute for that Nature? I do not know, unless it be the Church of England. . . . The love of Nature and fullest perception of the revelation which she is to man is not compatible with the belief in the peculiar revelation of the Bible which Ruskin entertains." (*W*, XVI, 147).

This journal entry was made in 1857, but Thoreau's attitude on the subject was already well-formed by 1841:

> In reading a work on agriculture, I skip the author's moral reflections, and the words "Providence" and "He" scattered along the page, to come at the profitable level of what he has to say. There is no science in men's religion; it does not teach me so much as the report of the committee on swine. My author shows he has dealt in corn and turnips and can worship God with the hoe and spade, but spare me his morality. (*W*, VII, 243)

When Thoreau sharpened this passage for inclusion in *A Week*, he felt strongly enough about the matter to illustrate his spleen by adding a potent metaphor in the middle of the paragraph: "What he calls his religion is for the most part offensive to the nostrils. He should know better than expose himself, and keep his foul sores covered till they are quite healed" (*W*, I, 79). The point is somewhat uncomfortably overstressed (one begins to understand the failure of *A Week*), but we are at least made aware of the strength of Thoreau's prejudice on the subject. The books he wanted were those like Evelyn's *Silva*—which Thoreau, alluding ironically (as he

does in *Walden*) to the Shorter Catechism, called "a new kind
of prayerbook, a glorifying of the trees and enjoying them
forever, which was the chief end of his life" (*W*, X, 85)—or
the Homeric poems:

> The Iliad is not Sabbath but morning reading, and men cling
> to this old song, because they have still moments of unbaptized
> and uncommitted life which give them an appetite for more.
> There is no cant in him [Homer], as there is no religion. (*W*,
> VII, 284)

The best art, Thoreau implied, is "unbaptized"—at least morally indifferent, and perhaps even reprehensible in that, far
from weaning us from the world, it develops in us an aug-
mented appetite for life. The true writer, he suggested in a
journal entry for 1841, will never cheat his audience with a
cheap didacticism:

> The best thought is not only without sombreness, but even
> without morality. The universe lies outspread in floods of
> white light to it. The moral aspect of nature is a jaundice
> reflected from man. To the innocent there are no cherubim
> nor angels. Occasionally we rise above the necessity of virtue
> into an unchangeable morning light, in which we have not to
> choose in a dilemma between right and wrong, but simply to
> live right on and breathe the circumambient air. There is no
> name for this life unless it be the very vitality of *vita*. Silent is
> the preacher about this, and silent must ever be, for he who
> knows it will not preach. (*Ibid.*, 265)

To catch "the very vitality of *vita*"—this was to be Thoreau's
program as a writer, a program which specifically excluded
moral reference from his writing. Nor was this resolution idly
taken; Thoreau would complain in 1842 of his lapses from
grace: "What offends me most in my compositions is the moral
element in them. . . . Those undeserved joys which come
uncalled and make us more pleased than grateful are they that

sing" (*Ibid.*, 316). These are hardly the words of a writer who would build his style on a theory of Transcendental Correspondence.

The "true and absolute account of things" (*W*, IX, 103–4), then, that Thoreau would attempt was the outcome of a perception of moral relativity more thoroughgoing than that which led Emerson to relegate Christ, with only slightly diminished respect, to the "true race of prophets" (*C*, I, 128). Not only was Thoreau unwilling to admit man's divine destiny ("The gods are of no sect; they side with no man" [*W*, VII, 249]); he was not even prepared to espouse the "certain divine laws" (*C*, I, 121)—the moral sentiment—onto which Emerson fell back:

> The infinite bustle of Nature of a summer's noon, or her infinite silence of a summer's night, gives utterance to no dogma. They do not say to us even with a seer's assurance, that this or that law is immutable and so ever and only can the universe exist. But they are the indifferent occasion for all things and the annulment of all laws. (*W*, VII, 133)

This was Thoreau in his journal for 1840, preparing himself, one feels, to level his opponents in the "Sunday" section of *A Week*, which was certainly meant less as a specifically anti-Christian and anti-religious polemic than as a plea for catholicity in religious opinions and attitudes:

> The wisest man preaches no doctrines; he has no scheme; he sees no rafter, not even a cobweb, against the heavens. It is clear sky. If I ever see more clearly at one time than at another, the medium through which I see is clearer. To see from earth to heaven, and see there standing, still a fixture, that old Jewish scheme! What right have you to hold up this obstacle to my understanding you, to your understanding me! You did not invent it; it was imposed on you. Examine your authority. . . . Your scheme must be the framework of the universe; all other schemes will soon be ruins. The perfect

God in his revelations of himself has never got to the length of one such proposition as you, his prophets, state. . . . Can you put mysteries into words? Do you presume to fable of the ineffable? (*W*, I, 70–71)

In *Nature* Emerson had, of course, stated unequivocally that nature echoes the Ten Commandments. Thoreau, in his first book, was evidently responding to his mentor. If true religious revelations are ineffable, Thoreau seems to have been asking, how could the Transcendentalists be so certain of the symbolic correspondence between the real and the spiritual? "The poet," he wrote in 1840, "does not need to see how meadows are something else than earth, grass, and water, but how they are thus much" (*W*, VII, 114). Correspondence attempts to divert our attention beyond the visible reality; Thoreau was determined to stick with the thing-in-itself.

The common view of Thoreau, which sees him as a disciple of Emerson and states that he regarded "the material world as a symbol of the spiritual," was undoubtedly largely promulgated by Emerson himself in his biographical sketch of Thoreau.[25] The older Transcendentalist certainly did it in all innocence and sincerity; that was simply how he saw his young friend. But many of the key statements in Emerson's essay can be refuted by excerpts from Thoreau's own writings, almost as if the latter had feared misrepresentation and provided a defense against it in advance. Emerson, for instance, wrote of Thoreau: "The depth of his perception found likeness of law throughout Nature, and I know not any genius who so swiftly inferred universal law from the single fact" (*C*, X, 474). Thoreau, however, in 1851 had written in his journal: "Ah, give me pure mind, pure thought! Let me not be in haste to detect the *universal law*; let me see more clearly a particular instance of it!" (*W*, IX, 157).

Ten years earlier Thoreau had made the following subtle distinction: "It is more proper for a spiritual fact to have suggested an analogous natural one, than for the natural fact to have preceded the spiritual in our minds" (*W*, VII, 175). Thoreau's notion, which is suggestive of modern poetic theory, is that a writer should seek out a proper "correlative object" from the real world by which his thought may be represented.[26] In Thoreau's view, the natural fact does not (to borrow Emerson's words) "hint or thunder to man" (*C*, I, 40–1) the unique spiritual law for which, according to the Transcendentalists, it is supposed to stand. "My thought," Thoreau wrote in 1852, "is a part of the meaning of the world, and hence I use a part of the world as a symbol to express my thought" (*W*, X, 410). The world, Thoreau implies, comes first and contains all things in it, including the thinking creatures that it brings forth; it is not a servant merely standing in for its Platonic master. Emerson, however, attributed to Thoreau exactly the opposite view: ". . . there was an excellent wisdom in him, proper to a rare class of men, which showed him the material world as a means and symbol" (*C*, X, 464). Apparently Emerson had not read *A Week* with sufficient care to notice Thoreau's specific objection to this notion: "Are we to be put off and amused in this life, as it were with a mere allegory? Is not Nature, rightly read, that of which she is commonly taken to be the symbol merely?" (*W*, I, 408).

The created universe *is* the reality, Thoreau was arguing, and the Correspondential attitude toward nature cheats us with a pious fiction. As for Emerson's allegation in *Nature* that "sensible objects conform to the premonitions of Reason and reflect the conscience" (*C*, I, 40), Thoreau was simply not concerned with the conscience: "The conscience really does not, and ought not to monopolize the whole of our lives, any more than the heart or the head. It is as liable to disease as any other part" (*W*, I, 75). Furthermore, if, as seemed clear, Emerson's Over-Soul turned out to be simply another name for Duty, the divine, in Thoreau's view, was certainly being rather narrowly defined: "It seems to me that the god that is commonly worshiped in civilized countries is not at all divine, though he bears a divine name, but is the overwhelming authority and respectability of mankind combined. Men reverence one another, not yet God" (*Ibid.*, 65–66). The spiritual world, of which, in Emerson's system, nature was no more than the symbol, seemed to Thoreau to be the apotheosis of ethics. Such a view might serve as moral philosophy, but he was convinced that it could hardly be adequate as religion. And for all the affection between him and Emerson, the tragically important fact remained that they simply did not worship in the same way: "Ah, I yearn toward thee, my friend, but I have not confidence in thee. We do not believe in the same God."

IV

It would be convenient, for this discussion, to consider Thoreau's *Walden*—by common consent, his one perfect work—to be the expression of his slowly developing decision to extricate himself from the morass of questions on the infinite and eternal that his Transcendental brethren had so long and so earnestly been asking. Thoreau certainly does declare in *Walden* that, in the face of the created universe, such questions are impertinent:

> After a still winter night I awoke with the impression that some question had been put to me, which I had been endeavoring in vain to answer in my sleep, as what—how—when—where? But there was dawning Nature, in whom all creatures live, looking in at my broad windows with serene and satisfied face, and no question on *her* lips. I awoke to an answered question, to Nature and daylight. The snow lying deep on the earth dotted with young pines, and the very slope of the hill on which my house is placed, seemed to say, Forward! Nature puts no question and answers none which we mortals ask. She has long ago taken her resolution. (*W*, II, 312)

But Thoreau had taken his resolution on these matters long before *Walden* was published. He began his career as a disciple of Emerson not so much because he was thoroughly convinced on all the major points of Emerson's philosophy as for reasons of propinquity and necessity. Emerson lived in Concord and was sympathetic, wise, and famous; and every thoughtful and ambitious young man needs a model. But Thoreau's own genius, his particular way of looking at the universe and peculiar solution of the problem of redefining religious experience in mid-nineteenth-century America, is apparent in his earliest writings, as in the following journal entry for 1838:

> We may believe it, but never do we live a quiet, free life, such as Adam's, but are enveloped in an invisible network of speculations. Our progress is only from one such speculation to another, and only at rare intervals do we perceive that it is no progress. Could we for a moment drop this by-play, and simply wonder, without reference or inference! (*W*, VII, 61)

The youthful élan of this entry may ignore the difficulties that the decidedly post-Adamic Thoreau would encounter in his self-constituted Arcadia. But we are at least presented with a fair statement of Thoreau's intent: simple wonder—an attempt at continued amazement and ecstasy over the physical conditions of man's existence—without the Correspondential "reference or inference" of which the other Transcendentalists were so fond. Their persistent desire for metaphysical knowledge he would claim not to share:

> My desire for knowledge is intermittent, but my desire to bathe my head in atmospheres unknown to my feet is perennial and constant. The highest that we can attain to is not Knowledge, but Sympathy with Intelligence. I do not know that this higher knowledge amounts to anything more definite than a novel and grand surprise on a sudden revelation of the insufficiency of all that we called Knowledge before,—a discov-

ery that there are more things in heaven and earth than are
dreamed of in our philosophy. It is the lighting up of the mist
by the sun. Man cannot *know* in any higher sense than this,
any more than he can look serenely and with impunity in the
face of the sun . . . (*W*, V, 240)

If Thoreau's "Sympathy with Intelligence" sounded oddly like
a mystical union which yielded a sensation but no definite
information, how could it appeal to his fellow Transcendentalists, for whom religion was largely a matter of ethics
and who certainly wanted to come away from their illuminated
moments with some sort of knowledge? Indeed, perhaps a large
source of the difficulty between Thoreau and the other Transcendentalists was semantic: they were using the same terms
with very different connotations. Thoreau's letter of April 3,
1850, to his disciple H. G. O. Blake, for instance, seems to be
an attempt at answering Blake's questions about the Supreme
Being:

> Let God alone if need be. Methinks, if I loved him more, I
> should keep him—I should keep myself rather,—at a more
> respectful distance. It is not when I am going to meet him, but
> when I am just turning away and leaving him alone, that I
> discover that God is. I say, God. I am not sure that that is the
> name. You will know whom I mean.[27]

One suspects that Blake, who was certainly Thoreau's most
sympathetic correspondent, did in fact know. But it is doubtful
whether Isaiah T. Williams, the young Buffalo lawyer whose
letters to Thoreau are a combination of pathos and treacle,
really understood what Thoreau meant when he wrote in
1841: "Our religion is where our love is."[28] Williams' religious quest was more metaphysical; he wished "to know mi-
nutely" about death and related matters.[29] But Thoreau's religious "love" was open to broader interpretation, as he intimates
in *A Week:* "There is in my nature, methinks, a singular

yearning toward all wildness. I know of no redeeming qualities in myself but a sincere love for some things, and when I am reproved I fall back on to this ground" (*W*, I, 54; cf. *W*, VII, 296).

Thoreau's love of wild things was at least morally ambiguous, if not potentially dangerous: a life of sensations rather than thoughts. "Why always insist that men incline to the moral side of their being?" he asked in 1840. "Our life is not all moral" (*W*, VII, 140). Perhaps, then, Charles Lane and Bronson Alcott were not entirely without foundation, at least in their own terms, when they insisted at the "Conversation" that Henry's love of nature was "the most subtle and dangerous of sins." It would lead Thoreau to write a curious chapter on "Higher Laws" in *Walden*, in which mention of a savage lust to devour a raw woodchuck or a fried rat, and the necessity of holiness in urination, play a strange counterpoint around a discussion of chastity and total purity. Thoreau's mixing of the wild and the good was certainly purposeful: the Transcendentalists' attitude toward nature was too tame, too involved with laws and society, for his taste:

I love Nature partly *because* she is not man, but a retreat from him. None of his institutions control or pervade her. There a different kind of right prevails. In her midst I can be glad with an entire gladness. If this world were all man, I could not stretch myself, I should lose all hope. He is constraint, she is freedom to me. He makes me wish for another world. She makes me content with this. None of the joys she supplies is subject to his rules and definitions. What he touches he taints. In thought he moralizes. One would think that no free, joyful labor was possible to him. How infinite and pure the least pleasure of which Nature is basis, compared with the congratulation of mankind! . . . Methinks that these prosers, with their saws and their laws, do not know how glad a man can be. What wisdom, what warning, can prevail against gladness?

There is no law so strong which a little gladness may not transgress. I have a room all to myself; it is nature. It is a place beyond the jurisdiction of human government. Pile up your books, the records of sadness, your saws and your laws. Nature is glad outside, and her merry worms within will ere long topple them down. There is a prairie beyond your laws. Nature is a prairie for outlaws. (W, X, 445–46)

Certainly this "outlaw" (like the devil's child that Emerson never was) saw no reason to turn Mirabeau (cf. W, II, 355) and take to the highway. It was sufficient in Thoreau's time and place to profess a philosophy of total "gladness" to be considered some sort of criminal. Indeed, it was simply this insistence on the radical importance of joy that separated Thoreau so widely from his fellow Transcendentalists: the one wanted ecstasy, the others ethics.

Thus, when H. G. O. Blake wrote Thoreau in 1848 claiming that he desired regeneration but shivered on the brink, the only advice Thoreau could deliver with sincerity was exactly what he had been telling himself for years in his journal:

I have no designs on society—or nature—or God. I am simply what I am, or I begin to be that. I *live* in the *present*. I only remember the past—and anticipate the future. I love to live, I love reform better than its modes. . . .

Pursue, keep up with, circle round and round your life as a dog does his master's chaise. Do what you love. Know your own bone; gnaw at it, bury it, unearth it, and gnaw it [still. Do not be too] moral. You may cheat yourself out of much life so. Aim above morality. Be not *simply* good—be good for something.—All fables indeed have their morals, but the innocent enjoy the story.[30]

It is surely no exaggeration to say that what Thoreau here offered Blake was startling enough to be the basis of an American aesthetic revolution of 1848, had Thoreau had any influence or a considerable following. Whitman, whose *Leaves of Grass* was to appear seven years later, inevitably comes to mind in connection with Thoreau's insistence on amoral ecstasy. But Emerson's influence on Whitman was much more pervasive and lasting than any effect he may have had on Thoreau. In Whitman the pure poetry of existence is too often obscured by a haze of unprecipitated ideas; one can only agree with Santayana that "the temperament is finer than the ideas and the poet wiser than the thinker." [31] Nevertheless, Whitman and Thoreau probably have more in common, finally, with each other than either does with Emerson. For both Whitman and Thoreau, Transcendentalism was a Saturnalia of sense experience. Unlike Emerson, who stood in awe before the "mighty and transcendent Soul" (*C*, I, 221), Thoreau trembled before the mystery of matter, of sheer physical existence:

> This was that Earth of which we have heard, made out of Chaos and Old Night. Here was no man's garden, but the unhandseled globe. . . . Man was not to be associated with it. It was Matter, vast, terrific,—not his Mother Earth that we have heard of. . . . There was clearly felt the presence of a force not bound to be kind to man. . . . I stand in awe of my body, this matter to which I am bound has become so strange to me. I fear not spirits, ghosts, of which I am one,—*that* my body might,—but I fear bodies, I tremble to meet them. What is this Titan that has possession of me? Talk of mysteries! Think of our life in nature,—daily to be shown matter, to come in contact with it,—rocks, trees, wind on our cheeks! the *solid* earth! the *actual* world! the *common sense! Contact! Contact! Who* are we? *where* are we? (*W*, III, 78–79)

The strident tone of Thoreau's demand for union with physical reality seems here almost to defy the ordinary resources of typography for its full expression. His desire to grind himself into the earth was indeed, as Channing noted shrewdly, a devouring of himself alive—for, once in full contact with the world, how would Thoreau distinguish between his sensations and their cause? At any rate, given his motives, it is clear why Thoreau's separation from his fellow Transcendentalists had to be so complete. As he wrote to Blake in his letter of March 27, 1848, "In what concerns you much do not think that you have companions—know that you are alone in the world." [32] The search for ecstasy is a lonely occupation, because of both its necessary means and its inevitable conclusion: as Thoreau knew only too well, the end of physical joy is decay and death. He would, however, attempt to elude the ordinary consequences of sensualism by turning his deification of the five senses into a theory of art.

CHAPTER SIX

Thoreau's Aesthetic:

A Purely Sensuous Life

I

IT was Ralph Waldo Emerson who wrote of his friend Henry Thoreau that "few lives contain so many renunciations," that Thoreau had "no appetites, no passions" (C, X, 454). He implied thereby that even he himself had a greater zest for the ordinary components of life than his naysaying and fastidious disciple. But Thoreau's unequivocal "I love to live" [1] seems a more clearly passionate statement about existence than Emerson's curiously qualified remarks on the subject:

> The life lived, the thing done is a paltry & drivelling affair, as far as I know it, though in the presence & consciousness of the magnificent, yea the unspeakably great. Yet I love life—never little,—and now, I think, more & more, entertained & puzzled though I be by this lubricity of it, & inaccessibleness of its pith & heart. The variety of our vital game delights me. [2]

Emerson wrote this to Margaret Fuller in 1843, in his fortieth year. It appears to be the expression of a disillusioned spirit, a spectator at the game of life, enough amused by the vanity of the world to be willing to oversee it but not really to participate in it. Five years later, in a letter to Caroline Sturgis Tappan, Emerson admitted that even the "variety of our vital game" had failed him:

The universe is all chemistry, with a certain hint of a
magnificent *Whence* or *Whereto* gilding or opalizing every
angle of the old salt-acid acid-salt, endlessly reiterated &
masqueraded thro' all time & space & form. The addition of
that hint everywhere, saves things. Heavy & loathsome is the
bounded world, bounded everywhere.[3]

How much a child of New England Emerson here shows
himself to be! Not only do most things break; they were not
really valuable to begin with. The world is heavy and loathsome, and the only thing that mitigates this dreary picture for
Emerson is the "magnificent *Whence* or *Whereto*," specifically
referred to in this letter as Fate—the Beautiful Necessity, that
"breath of will" which "blows eternally through the universe of
souls in the direction of the Right and Necessary" (*C*, VI,
27–28). For Emerson, then, love of life meant largely love of
the eternal laws which he found symbolized by the phenomenal world. Things in themselves were dust and ashes.

Thoreau, on the other hand, in his forty-first year, could
write of the bounded world in a much different spirit:

You must love the crust of the earth on which you dwell more
than the sweet crust of any bread or cake. You must be able to
extract nutriment out of a sandheap. You must have so good
an appetite as this, else you will live in vain. (*W*, XVI, 258)

For Thoreau the world was not a pasteboard mask hiding the
golden Over-Soul, but a place "worthy to inhabit" (*W*, IX,
485), the very *prima materia*—"the solid and sunny earth, the
basis of all philosophy, and poetry, and religion even" (*Ibid.*,
327). The one appetite that Emerson had plainly overlooked in
describing Thoreau was the latter's insatiable taste for earth.
"Such an appetite have we for new life," Thoreau wrote in
1859, "that we begin by nibbling the very crust of the earth"
(*W*, XVIII, 113). The metaphor was not a mere mannerism:
he simply thought of natural objects in terms of food, as in
"Chesuncook," where he tells us that the sight of fir, spruce,

and evergreen trees was for him "like the sight and odor of cake to a schoolboy" (*W*, III, 95). And contact with the earth—indeed, immersion in it, he insisted—was his unavoidable starting point. He could, in 1840, humorously call it "a luxury to stand up to one's chin in some retired swamp for a whole summer's day" (*W*, VII, 141). But the significance of this comi-tragic activity (the image of Thoreau, our knowledge of his consumption) is underlined by a journal entry nineteen years later: "Nature, the earth herself, is the only panacea. They bury poisoned sheep up to their necks in earth to take the poison out of them" (*W*, XVIII, 350). Thoreau would try to make burial the source of life before it became the terminus required by death.

But although Thoreau was certainly conscious of his own stratagem, his sheer love of the world clearly takes precedence over his need to anticipate death by cherishing the earth. Of course, the two things could frequently co-exist, as in this journal entry inspired by a trip to Lake Cochituate:

> Dear to me to lie in, this sand; fit to preserve the bones of a race for thousands of years to come. And this is my home, my native soil; and I am a New-Englander. Of thee, O earth, are my bone and sinew made; to thee, O sun, am I brother. . . . To this dust my body will gladly return as to its origin. Here have I my habitation. I am of thee. (*W*, IX, 95)

Still, what impresses us here is Thoreau's genuine pride in his country, a pride too frequently expressed to be ignored:

> The delicious soft, spring-suggesting air,—how it fills my veins with life! Life becomes again credible to me. A certain dormant life awakes in me, and I begin to love nature again. Here is my Italy, my heaven, my New England. (*W*, XIII, 104–5)

New England is worthy to inhabit, to love, and to make art out of, but not New England as abstraction—New England as earth and vegetation. So Thoreau invests the very trees with personality: "How full of life and of eyes is the damp bark! It would not be worth the while to die and leave all this life behind one" (*Ibid.*, 105). The irony is compressed and subtle: we must, of course, die and leave all this life behind, but it would not be worth-while to live without having experienced to the utmost what we must leave. For Thoreau tragic love presupposes both deep attachment and necessary renunciation; and art flourishes on this tragic perception.

Thoreau's passion for the earth, then, was to be the basis of a perfectly self-reliant attempt at the artistic life by a man who believed that "here or nowhere is our heaven" (*W*, I, 405). While his Transcendental brethren were laboring over the "*spiritual* phenomena of the day," Thoreau found for himself a "*phaenogamous* subject" (*W*, IX, 326–27): he would study not the relation of the soul to the body, but the relation of his body to the material world. And by virtue of this experiment in individual ecstasy turned into art, Thoreau would constitute himself New England's first notable aesthete.

II

"Shall I not have intelligence with the earth?" Thoreau asked in *Walden*, "Am I not partly leaves and vegetable mould myself?" (*W*, II, 153). His question was by no means simply a rhetorical pose, the vaunt of a self-conscious Romantic poet at his having succeeded in escaping from the corrupt city to innocent nature. At a time when so many of his fellow thinkers and writers were reaching out for the infinite and the eternal by trying to abstract themselves from earth, Thoreau was involved in demonstrating how wrong Emerson was in saying that "an idealist can never go backward to be a materialist" (*C*, I, 330). An idealist, Thoreau argued, *must* begin as a materialist, for the material universe is the only sane basis of all art, philosophy, and religion. But as Thoreau quickly added: "We

may live the life of a plant or an animal, without living an
animal life" (*W*, VII, 326). "Nature," as Santayana notes, "is
material, but not materialistic." [4]

So Thoreau's quaint insistence on the earth (was he not,
after all, a Transcendentalist?) was partially a stratagem of
insinuation: a way of suggesting that he was a materialist
—that materialism was necessary—without gathering to himself the opprobrium which, in the Concord circle, an open
avowal of that philosophical position would certainly have
earned. His attitude would often be expressed humorously, in
the punning fashion that he never tired of: "I love nature, I
love the landscape, because it is so sincere. It never cheats me.
It never jests. . . . I lie and relie [*sic*] on the earth" (*W*, VIII,
100). Or he could poke gentle fun at Transcendental idealism,
in the process of expressing his own position, by writing of a
mud turtle in the way in which someone else might write of the
Over-Soul:

> When I awake in the morning, I remember what I have seen
> and heard of snapping turtles, and am in doubt whether it was
> dream or reality. I slowly raise my head and peeping over the
> bedside see my great mud turtle shell lying bottom up under
> the table, showing its prominent ribs, and realize into what
> world I have awakened. Before I was in doubt how much
> prominence my good Genius would give to that fact. That the
> first object you see on awakening should be an empty mud
> turtle's shell!! Will it not make me of the earth earthy? Or does
> it not indicate that I am of the earth earthy? . . . When I see
> this, then I am sure that I am not dreaming, but am awake to
> this world. I do not know any more terrene fact. It still carries
> the earth on its back. (*W*, XII, 478–79)

"The Imagination," Keats once wrote, "may be compared to
Adam's dream—he awoke and found it truth." [5] Thoreau's
dream is not of some transcendent reality, but of a natural fact;
and when the imagination is kept within earthy bounds, dream

and reality are one. "We can conceive of nothing more fair," Thoreau wrote in *A Week,* "than something which we have experienced" (*W,* I, 406). His obsessive concern with remaining "of the earth earthy" simply arose out of a belief that the imagination, if it is not to cheat, must flower from actual experience.

Indeed, implicit in Thoreau's tireless insistence that man be "naturalized, on the soil of earth" (*Ibid.,* 405), is a total skepticism about traditional religious assumptions—the kinds of "ideals" which, in nonsectarian and Platonic terms, most of the Transcendentalists still held to. "God," Emerson wrote in 1848, "is a reality and his method is illusion" (*J,* VII, 505). Thoreau, however, was thoroughly content (in the words of Wallace Stevens) to "let be be finale of seem." [6] What Emerson considered mere illusion was sufficient reality for Thoreau: "the facts of life—the vital facts, which are the phenomena or actuality the gods meant to show us" (*W,* VII, 362). To Thoreau nature was not only phenomenal, as Emerson claimed, but both phenomenal *and* substantial. Thoreau was therefore largely committed to a philosophy of surfaces:

> I live so much in my habitual thoughts, a routine of thought, that I forget there is any outside to the globe, and am surprised when I behold it as now. . . . it is salutary to deal with the surface of things. . . . There is something invigorating in this air, which I am peculiarly sensible is a real wind, blowing from over the surface of a planet. I look out at my eyes, I come to my window, and I feel and breathe the fresh air. It is a fact equally glorious with the most inward experience. Why have we ever slandered the outward? The perception of surfaces will always have the effect of miracle to a sane sense. (*W,* X, 312–13)

"Olympus," he wrote in the following year (1853), "is the outside of the earth everywhere" (*W,* XI, 200). The earth is that divine surface which, acting upon the soul of man—those "divine germs called the senses" (*W*, I, 408)—produces Thoreau's miracle:

> It is the marriage of the soul with Nature that makes the intellect fruitful, that gives birth to imagination. When we were dead and dry as the highway, some sense which has been healthily fed will put us in relation with Nature, in sympathy with her; some grains of fertilizing pollen, floating in the air, fall on us, and suddenly the sky is all one rainbow, is full of music and fragrance and flavor. (*W*, VIII, 413)

Thoreau insisted on his kinship with the material universe, his being "a child of the earth" (*W*, XIX, 144), because it was the *sine qua non* of his experience. And his credo consisted mainly of two elements—world and sense:

> I wish so to live ever as to derive my satisfactions and inspirations from the commonest events, every-day phenomena, so that what my senses hourly perceive, my daily walk, the conversation of my neighbors, may inspire me, and I may dream of no heaven but that which lies about me. (*W*, XIV, 204)

realist?

In Thoreau one finds no exalted distinctions made between Reason and Understanding, as in Emerson. In fact, Thoreau's use of the term *reason* was generally traditional—"It is best that reason should govern us, and not these blind intimations, in which we exalt our fears into a genius" (*W*, VIII, 380)—and he was usually willing to remain within what Emerson called "the low circle of the senses and the understanding" (*J*, X, 115). Thoreau had nothing to say for innate ideas, eternal and immutable principles either pre-existent in the mind or grasped intuitively from above. And the dictum, which was anathema to Emerson and his followers, that there is "nothing in the intellect which was not previously in the experience of the senses" (*C*, I, 340), can stand as a fair representation of Thoreau's position. Indeed, it is finally worth suggesting that, in Thoreau, the other Transcendentalists were unknowingly harboring a Lockean in their midst.[7]

We have already noted that on ethical grounds Locke and Emerson were substantially in agreement. But this was generally overlooked at the time because most Transcendentalists were so distressed by the Lockean psychology. The word *sense* was a red flag. It was associated with the official Unitarian theology they despised (especially that of Andrews Norton, with his insistence on the historical verifiability of everything contained in the Gospels). It stood for a world in which well-being counted for more than timeless moral imperatives; it conjured up the vulgar pleasure-pain principles of a Bentham; and finally, as Emerson argued while attacking Locke in *English Traits,* the sense philosophy was the opposite of the "poetic tendency": " 'Tis quite certain that . . . the dull men will be Lockists" (C, V, 239). Thus Emerson could complain in his journal for 1853:

> The English mind now is superstitious before facts, facts, they make a great ado about a truth . . . no deep *aperçu,* no all-binding theory, no glimpse of distant relations, and the *quoddam vinculum.* There is poor-smell, and learned trifling, and Locke instead of Berkeley. (*J,* VIII, 417–18)

The "all-binding theory" which Emerson wanted was poetic and abstract, not wedded to facts. Thoreau, as we have noted, had an aversion to abstractions and a peculiar attachment to facts. Indeed, just before Thoreau's arrival in May 1843 at William Emerson's house on Staten Island, Emerson wrote ahead to warn his brother of Thoreau's "village exaggeration of the value of facts." [8] But addiction to facts, we may note in retrospect, was hardly the worst of it. What would Emerson have said if he had suspected Thoreau of being a "sensationalist"? By the commonest standards of the Transcendental movement, that is exactly what Thoreau was. George Bancroft,

for instance, in his *History of the United States,* made a
standard distinction: "Locke sought truth through the senses
and the outward world; Penn looked inward to the divine
revelations in every mind." [9] It is easy to note where Thoreau
stood. Again, some of Bancroft's remarks in *The Boston Quarterly Review* for October 1838 offer an opportunity for even
sharper comparison:

> The five senses do not constitute the whole inventory of our
> sources of knowledge. They are the organs by which thought
> connects itself with the external universe; but the power of
> thought is not merged in the exercise of its instruments. We
> have functions which connect us with heaven, as well as
> organs which set us in relation with earth. [10]

For Thoreau there was no distinction between the "functions
which connect us with heaven" and the "organs which set us in
relation with earth," as is made abundantly clear in *A Week:*

> We need pray for no higher heaven than the pure senses can
> furnish, a *purely* sensuous life. Our present senses are but the
> rudiments of what they are destined to become. We are
> comparatively deaf and dumb and blind, and without smell or
> taste or feeling. Every generation makes the discovery that its
> divine vigor has been dissipated, and each sense and faculty
> misapplied and debauched. The ears were made, not for such
> trivial uses as men are wont to suppose, but to hear celestial
> sounds. The eyes were not made for such groveling uses as
> they are now put to and worn out by, but to behold beauty
> now invisible. May we not *see* God? (*W*, I, 408)

By "beauty now invisible" Thoreau meant (as did Keats and
Shelley [11]), not something abstract and inward, but what was
actually apparent, though overlooked by most. Poets *see;* other
people only look. As for John Locke, poet or not, Thoreau
never saw fit in his writings to attack him, probably because it
never occurred to him to do so. But it would have been difficult

in any case: Locke was Thoreau's philosophical father, as he
has been of many another poet.

Thoreau's outlook was strongly dependent on the life of the
five senses. Virtue for him was synonymous with the purity of
the senses; and he defined health, both physical and mental, in
exactly the same fashion: "In health all the senses receive
enjoyment and each seeks its own gratification.—it is a pleasure to see, and to walk, and to hear—&c." [12] He was convinced
that "to see the sun rise or go down every day would preserve us
sane forever" (W, IX, 208; cf. XII, 329) and that true
depression of spirits was impossible for the *pure* sensualist:
"There can be no really black melan-choly to him who lives in
the midst of nature and has still his senses" (W, VII, 364).
Predictably, Thoreau's over-all advice on living arose from the
same source as his definitions of health and virtue:

> We do not commonly live our life out and full; we do not fill
> all our pores with our blood; we do not inspire and expire fully
> and entirely enough, so that the wave, the comber, of each
> inspiration shall break upon our extremest shores, rolling till it
> meets the sand which bounds us, and the sound of the surf
> come back to us. Might not a bellows assist us to breathe? That
> our breathing should create a wind in a calm day! We live but
> a fraction of our life. Why do we not let on the flood, raise the
> gates, and set all our wheels in motion? He that hath ears to
> hear, let him hear. Employ your senses. (W, VIII, 251)

If the message is at first swallowed up in the turbulence of the
metaphor, the simplicity of Thoreau's last sentence is admirably clear. He could, however, turn biblical exegete and
deliver the same text in terms utterly familiar to New England
ears (including his own):

> Remember thy Creator in the days of thy youth; *i.e.,* lay up a
> store of natural influences. Sing while you may, before the
> evils days come. He that hath ears, let him hear. See, hear,

smell, taste, etc., while these senses are fresh and pure. (*Ibid.*, 330)

Unlike the Preacher, Thoreau did not advocate the fear of God as man's primary responsibility. "The whole duty of man," he wrote in 1840, "may be expressed in one line,— Make to yourself a perfect body" (*W*, VII, 147). However Thoreau arranged his sermon, it always came out the same: "A man should feed his senses with the best that the land affords" (*W*, VIII, 496). And such magic words of the Transcendental movement as *genius* and *inspiration*—so frequently identified by Emerson and others with the Over-Soul and the eternal—were defined by Thoreau in his peculiarly mundane fashion:

> What is called genius is the abundance of life or health, so that whatever addresses the senses, as the flavor of these berries, or the lowing of that cow . . . each sight and sound and scent and flavor,—intoxicates with a healthy intoxication. (*W*, X, 218)

We are forever brought back to the realm of the senses: "To perceive freshly, with fresh senses, is to be inspired" (*W*, XIV, 44). Thoreau simply thought of abstractions, when he thought of them at all, in terms of possible experience: "How much virtue there is in simply seeing! . . . We are as much as we see. Faith is sight and knowledge" (*W*, VII, 247–48). His speculations were guided by the range of his five senses.

Indeed, so concerned was Thoreau with the senses that he was even loath to lump them together (except in a very special way) and devoted much space to precise anatomization of the particular virtues of each one, among which he almost always mentions its special affinity to the earth. Sight, for instance, which he once named the Brahmin caste of the five senses,[13] he could describe in a strikingly original metaphor: "If I am well, then I see well. The bulletins of health are twirled along my visual rays, like pasteboards on a kite string" (W, VII, 266). In many references to the eye, he takes the opportunity to chastise subtly the Transcendental desire to see into the empyrean: "The eye must be firmly anchored to this earth which beholds birches and pines waving in the breeze in a certain light, a serene rippling light" (Ibid., 351). He could even devise anatomical arguments to bolster his predilection for observing the commonplace:

> Man's eye is so placed as to look straight forward on a level best, or rather down than up. His eye demands the sober colors of the earth for its daily diet. He does not look up at a great angle but with an effort. (W, IX, 387)

Smell, however, seems to have been as dear to his heart as vision, and in a journal entry for 1852 he temporarily dethroned the latter in favor of the former, calling scent "a more primitive inquisition than the eye, more oracular and trustworthy. . . . By it I detect earthiness" (W, X, 40). This it was—its sensitivity to earthiness—for which he chiefly valued his ability to smell: "I love the rank smells of the swamp, its decaying leaves" (Ibid., 305). And on March 18, 1853, he devoted a whole paragraph to announcing dramatically: "To-day first I smelled the earth" (W, XI, 27). In another journal entry he mixed smell and taste in a metaphor of perfect contentment: "As I go home by Hayden's I smell the burning meadow. I love the scent. It is my pipe. I smoke the earth" (W, XII, 439-40). Sensation was total experience for Thoreau; the scent of apples, he noted in 1853, "affects me like a performance, a poem, a thing done" (W, XI, 328).

As with sight, smell, and taste, it is earthiness that Thoreau wants in his sound: "The creaking of the crickets seems at the very foundation of all sound. At last I cannot tell it from a ringing in my ears. . . . It reminds me that I am a denizen of the earth" (W, VIII, 306). The same is true of his sense of touch: "To the sane man the world is a musical instrument. The very touch affords an exquisite pleasure" (*Ibid.*, 269). For Thoreau man's grip on life is literally a tangible thing: "When I took the ether my consciousness amounted to this: I put my finger on myself in order to keep the place, otherwise I should never have returned to this world" (*W*, XIV, 142).

Thoreau is alive so long as he can feel himself in contact with the world; and it is just this desire for both specificity and totality of perception that allows him to lump his senses in the only way in which they will not lose their individuality—the unity of synesthesia:

> The trees, seen dimly through the mist, suggest things which do not at all belong to the past, but are peculiar to my fresh New England life. It is as novel as green peas. The dew hangs everywhere upon the grass, and I breathe the rich, damp air in slices. (*W*, VII, 267)

The careful confusion here of sight, smell, taste, and touch suggests Keats; and in another journal entry in which the senses are mixed, the Keatsian note is unmistakable:

> As my eye rested on the blossom of the meadowsweet in a hedge, I heard the note of an autumnal cricket, and was penetrated with the sense of autumn. Was it sound? or was it form? or was it scent? or was it flavor? It is now the royal month of August. When I hear this sound, I am as dry as the rye which is everywhere cut and housed, though I am drunk with the season's wine. (*W*, VIII, 370)

"O for a Life of Sensations rather than of Thoughts!" Keats wrote to Benjamin Bailey in 1817. "Oh, if I could be intoxicated on air and water!" Thoreau exclaimed to himself in 1850 (*Ibid.*, 72), anticipating by just a decade Emily Dickinson's "Inebriate of Air—am I—/And Debauchee of Dew." For all three, the drunkenness of pure sensation was synonymous with life, and the sobriety of a life without sense experience was but another name for the ever-threatening winter of death.

Indeed, Thoreau's intense annual distress at the approach of winter itself was not only the result of a symbolic anticipation of death; it was actually the time of year when the sources of life—the five senses—were least operative. Samuel Johnson was appalled at the thought that "we shall receive no letters in the grave"; [14] Thoreau, one feels, was horrified because death was the end of sensation. (There, perhaps, we have one large difference, at least in literary terms, between the eighteenth and nineteenth centuries.) Thoreau's journal entries for the beginning of winter are frequently bleak, such as this one for November 27, 1853: "Now a man will eat his heart, if ever, now while the earth is bare, barren and cheerless, and we have the coldness of winter without the variety of ice and snow" (W, XI, 520). Four years later he dubbed that month "November Eat-heart":

> Not only the fingers cease to do their office, but there is often a benumbing of the faculties generally. You can hardly screw up your courage to take a walk when all is thus tightly locked or frozen up and so little is to be seen in field or wood. (W, XVI, 203)

March was equally bad: "I run about these cold and blustering days, on the whole perhaps the worst to bear in the year,—partly because they disappoint expectation—looking almost in vain for some animal or vegetable life stirring" (W, XIII, 274). Two days later he concluded about both months that "he must have a great deal of life in him to draw upon, who can pick up a subsistence in November and March" (Ibid., 276). If it is true that character is most clearly exhibited in extreme conditions, Thoreau's entries for these marginal months should be particularly revelatory; and indeed this is what we find. The entry for November 13, 1851, for instance, seems a perfect illustration of the Thoreauvian method literally laid bare:

> A cold and dark afternoon, the sun being behind clouds in the west. The landscape is barren of objects, the trees being leafless, and so little light in the sky for variety. Such a day as will almost oblige a man to eat his own heart. A day in which you must hold on to life by your teeth. You can hardly ruck up any skin on Nature's bones. The sap is down; she won't peel. Now is the time to cut timber for yokes and ox-bows, leaving the tough bark on,—yokes for your own neck. Finding yourself yoked to Matter and to Time. Truly a hard day, hard times these! Not a mosquito left. Not an insect to hum. Crickets gone into winter quarters. Friends long since gone there, and you left to walk on frozen ground, with your hands in your pockets. Ah, but is not this a glorious time for your deep inward fires? And will not your green hickory and white oak burn clear in this frosty air? Now is not your manhood taxed by the great Assessor? Taxed for having a soul, a ratable soul. A day when you cannot pluck a flower, cannot dig a parsnip, nor pull a turnip, for the frozen ground! What do the thoughts find to live on? What avails you now the fire you stole from heaven? Does not each thought become a vulture to gnaw your vitals? (*W*, IX, 110-11)

Thoreau is faced with a hard day, a day without sensations. He carefully, even painfully, catalogs what there is available for each sense and comes up with nothing. The landscape is barren, the trees leafless, and the sky dark, so there is little to see; nature's bones are skinless ("she won't peel"), and it is difficult to feel; as for sound, the mosquitoes and crickets have deserted; and finally, flowers, parsnips, and turnips are gone, now that the ground is frozen, and there is nothing to smell or taste. In such a situation he at least tries to fall back on the "deep inward fires" dear to the hearts of all Transcendentalists, but he is forced to admit failure. Reflection—which, to the Lockean philosopher, is all that exists besides matter and

sensation—is simply the mind turning back on its own operations, so that each thought becomes "a vulture to gnaw your
vitals."

The desperate bleakness of Thoreau's life under such
conditions is made clear by contrast with another day, in
August of the same year, when the world was much different
and there was abundant food for all his senses:

> My heart leaps into my mouth at the sound of the wind in the
> woods. I, whose life was but yesterday so desultory and
> shallow, suddenly recover my spirits, my spirituality, through
> my hearing. . . . Ah, I would walk, I would sit and sleep,
> with natural piety! . . . For joy I could embrace the earth; I
> shall delight to be buried in it . . . now I have occasion to be
> grateful for the flood of life that is flowing over me. I am not so
> poor: I can smell the ripening apples; the very rills are deep;
> the autumnal flowers . . . feed my spirit, endear the earth to
> me, make me value myself and rejoice; the quivering of
> pigeons' wings reminds me of the tough fibre of the air which
> they rend. I thank you, God. I do not deserve anything, I am
> unworthy of the least regard; and yet I am made to rejoice. I
> am impure and worthless, and yet the world is gilded for my
> delight and holidays are prepared for me, and my path is
> strewn with flowers. . . . Ah, I would not tread on a cricket
> in whose song is such a revelation, so soothing and cheering to
> my ear! Oh, keep my senses pure! (*W*, VIII, 391–92)

The Wordsworthian echoes at the beginning of the passage are,
of course, not accidental; but it is important to note the
significant difference between the viewpoints of the two writers. For Wordsworth, since "nothing can bring back the
hour/Of splendour in the grass, of glory in the flower," he
must find his strength "in the faith that looks through
death,/In years that bring the philosophic mind." But Thoreau
has no desire to reconcile himself to the inevitable decay of his
faculties; and the hardships of winter have taught him not to

renounce his quest for sensation in preparation for death, but rather to await patiently the coming of spring. Wordsworth ends his "Ode" with a plea for philosophy; Thoreau can only beg: "Oh, keep my senses pure!"

Unlike Wordsworth, who believed the child blessed because of its still fresh intimations of immortality, Thoreau thought the child fortunate for reasons closer to Locke than to Plato: "The senses of children are unprofaned. Their whole body is one sense" (*W*, VIII, 291). In this journal entry for 1851 we undoubtedly have the source of the notion which Thoreau uses to begin the chapter on "Solitude" in *Walden*: "This is a delicious evening, when the whole body is one sense, and imbibes delight through every pore. I go and come with a strange liberty in Nature, a part of herself" (*W*, II, 143).

For Thoreau the great thing was unity of perception. "This is a world," he wrote in 1851, "where there are flowers" (*W*, VIII, 401); but flowers are of many sorts: "Flowers are the different colors of the sunlight" (*W*, XI, 185). In fact, in his journal he writes of rainbows, fruit, birds, stars, and even whole days themselves as if they were all flowers.[15] He apparently liked to think of the entire world as one huge plant: "The heavens and the earth are one flower. The earth is the calyx, the heavens the corolla" (*W*, XI, 225). Having envisioned all of nature as a single flower, Thoreau, like the Fabullus whom Catullus invited to dinner, could only pray that the gods would see fit to make him *totum nasum,* so that in one moment of perfect perception, he might sense the universe.

III

Thoreau, as opposed to Emerson, was not only an unconscious disciple of Locke; he was also an unwitting anti-Hegelian. Thoreau's belief in the primacy of the life of the senses made this situation inevitable. His cherished experience could only take place in a moment of time (the present moment) to a discrete consciousness (the simple, separate Henry Thoreau). Both of these conditions the philosophy of Hegel denied.

It would of course be absurd to speak of the direct influence, positive or negative, of the philosophy of Hegel on either of these men. What little of Hegel Emerson read came too late in life to affect his opinions; besides, he found Hegel a bore.[16] As for Thoreau, there is no evidence that he ever read a line of Hegel's. But what may for convenience be called the Hegelian position furnishes another opportunity for defining the differences between Thoreau's attitudes and Emerson's, as if nineteenth-century winds of doctrine had spontaneously blown the two men apart.

The primary reason for this division may be expressed in terms of the Hegelian notion of the "self," stated succinctly by Josiah Royce: "We have no life alone. There is no merely inner self. There is the world of selves. We live in our coherence with other people, in our relationships." [17] This appears to have been Emerson's position, even in the face of the seemingly egregious individualism of "Self-Reliance." Indeed, that very essay, with all its inconsistencies, demonstrates the thesis, as in the following characteristic passage, which, despite its initial self-contradiction, is clearly Hegelian in drift: [18]

> Trust thyself: every heart vibrates to that iron string. Accept the place the divine providence has found for you, the society of your contemporaries, the connection of events. Great men have always done so, and confided themselves childlike to the genius of their age, betraying their perception that the absolutely trustworthy was seated at their heart, working through their hands, predominating in all their being. And we are now men, and must accept in the highest mind the same transcendent destiny; and not minors and invalids in a protected corner, not cowards fleeing before a revolution, but guides,

redeemers and benefactors, obeying the Almighty effort and advancing on Chaos and the Dark. (C, II, 47)

But an even clearer parallel to Royce's statement can be found early in Emerson's career, in a journal entry for 1836: "Do you not see that a man is a bundle of relations, that his entire strength consists not in his properties, but in his innumerable relations?" (J, IV, 167). A quarter of a century later he reiterated this position while recording his agreement with Henry James, Sr.: [19]

> Another fine spiritual statement which he [James] made was to the effect that all which men value themselves for, as religious progress,—going alone, renouncing, and self-mortifying, to attain a certain religious superiority,—was the way *from*, not the way *to*, what they seek; for it is only as our existence is shared, not as it is selfhood, that it is divine. (J, IX, 297)

Society is ultimately the redeemed form of man, and duty calls us out of ourselves. But this, clearly, Thoreau was not willing to accede to. Not that he was opposed in principle to society or its institutional form, government. The American government's position on the Mexican War and slavery may have precipitated his attack on the State in "Civil Disobedience," but that essay is not a call to anarchy. Indeed, it ends by simply being a plea for freedom—for Thoreau—from any kind of relations:

> . . . the government does not concern me much, and I shall bestow the fewest possible thoughts on it. It is not many moments that I live under a government, even in this world. If a man is thought-free, fancy-free, imagination-free, that which *is not* never for a long time appearing *to be* to him, unwise rulers or reformers cannot fatally interrupt him. (W, IV, 383)

For Thoreau, shared existence was only the unfortunately necessary precondition of his selfhood. He could put up with it, but it was by no means *being*, as his most intense personal experience was: "Drifting in a sultry day on the sluggish waters of the pond, I almost cease to live and begin to be" (*W*, VII, 75). His political dream was finally a government which would leave him alone:

> I please myself with imagining a State at last which can afford to be just to all men, and to treat the individual with respect as a neighbor; which even would not think it inconsistent with its own repose if a few were to live aloof from it, not meddling with it, nor embraced by it, who fulfilled all the duties of neighbors and fellow-men. (*W*, IV, 387)

He saw his strength as consisting, not in "his innumerable relations," but in his precious personal properties, and he wished to be not so much in sharp opposition to society as simply set apart from it.

It was mainly the loss of the momentary harmonies of consciousness that Thoreau feared at the thought of being submerged in his relations: such a loss was equivalent to death. "But perhaps," he writes in the first chapter of *Walden*, "a man is not required to bury himself"; and he adds:

> . . . no doubt, they [the Hegelians?] have designs on us for our benefit, in making the life of a civilized people an *institution*, in which the life of the individual is to a great extent absorbed, in order to preserve and perfect that of the race. But I wish to show at what a sacrifice this advantage is at present obtained, and to suggest that we may possibly so live as to secure all the advantage without suffering any of the disadvantage. (*W*, II, 34–35)

Yet, of course, *in society* we cannot (nor could Thoreau) "so live" as to secure all the advantages of consciousness without suffering many disadvantages, and *Walden* is notoriously poor as a blueprint for improving society. (Thoreau's wry humor allowed him to perpetrate *that* joke.) The book is really a description of Thoreau's dream, to a large extent realized, of perfected self-indulgence and self-possession.

From another direction, we may notice Thoreau's reaction to the Hegelian conspiracy by glancing at his review of J. A. Etzler's *The Paradise within the Reach of all Men, without Labor, by Powers of Nature and Machinery. An Address to all intelligent Men.* In the first place, Thoreau's review is a slap at nineteenth-century notions of progress. Unlike Emerson, who seems finally to have believed in progress (on several occasions he mentions Etzler approvingly),[20] Thoreau's attitude was one of cosmic skepticism. In 1838 he wrote in his journal:

> Men have been contriving new means and modes of motion. Steamships have been westering during these late days and nights on the Atlantic waves,—the fuglers of a new evolution to this generation. Meanwhile plants spring silently by the brooksides, and the grim woods wave indifferent; the earth emits no howl, pot on fire simmers and seethes, and men go about their business. (*W*, VII, 43)

The eternal verities remain, and the universe is indifferent: change is not progress. The individual man achieves harmony or he does not, and this is always possible to the same degree. "What the first philosopher taught," Thoreau wrote in 1840, "the last will have to repeat. The *world* makes no progress" (*Ibid.,* 134). In his review he makes Etzler sound like a lunatic, escaped from Swift's Academy of Lagado, who is trying to extract, not sunshine from a cucumber, but mechanical bliss from sunshine. "The light of the sun is but the shadow of love," responds Thoreau, and love "can make a paradise within which will dispense with a paradise without" (*W*, IV, 304).

Etzler's belief in temporal progress is, moreover, not the only thing about his book that bothered Thoreau. The Hegelian note of nonexistence-out-of-combination is also clearly present in a passage of Etzler's which Thoreau quotes: " 'Man is powerful but in union with many. Nothing great, for the improvement of his own condition, or that of his fellow-men, can ever be effected by individual enterprise.' " Thoreau's retaliation is swift:

> Alas! this is the crying sin of the age, this want of faith in the prevalence of a man. Nothing can be effected but by one man. He who wants help wants everything. True, this is the condition of our weakness, but it can never be the means of our recovery. We must first succeed alone, that we may enjoy success together. (*Ibid.*, 299)

This response was predictable; what is particularly interesting about it is that, although Thoreau implies that social advancement can and will follow individual advancement, it is perfectly clear from his review that the kind of lonely success which he advocates simply cannot be shared. What Thoreau offers, a few pages further on, is private ecstasy (an Hegelian cipher):

> When the sunshine falls on the path of the poet, he enjoys all those pure benefits and pleasures which the arts slowly and partially realize from age to age. The winds which fan his cheek waft him the sum of that profit and happiness which their lagging inventions supply. (*Ibid.*, 302)

In his review, as in "Civil Disobedience" and *Walden,* Thoreau's "solution" to a social and political problem has very little to do with other people. It is really an angry vindication of his life as a poet. "He is the rich man and enjoys the fruits of riches," Thoreau wrote in 1841, "who, summer and winter forever, can find delight in the contemplation of his soul" (*W*, VII, 300). His ideal is personal; and his momentary illumination, "that morrow which mere lapse of time can never make to dawn" (*W*, II, 367), has nothing to do with the future.

Indeed, it is exactly this insistence on stasis—the present moment—that further separates Thoreau from the Hegelian position. For Hegel the present has no real existence: it is always and instantly decaying into the past and giving way to the future. As Royce puts it in his exegesis of Hegel, "Leave me alone to the self-consciousness of this moment, and I shrivel up into a mere atom, an unknowable feeling, a nothing." [21] Yet this Hegelian definition of nothingness—momentary self-consciousness—was for Thoreau the very essence of being. Emerson, in his essay "The Conservative," divided the world into the Party of the Past and the Party of the Future—Memory and Hope—but he left out the only party which would fit Thoreau, the Party of the Present. The "doctrine of this hour" (*W*, VII, 171) was to be a constant concern for Thoreau, and he would preach it to himself unceasingly:

> The present seems never to get its due; it is the least obvious,—neither before, nor behind, but within us. All the past plays into this moment, and we are what we are. My aspiration is one thing, my reflection another, but, over all, myself and condition is and does. (*Ibid.*, 190)

Aspiration and reflection—Emerson's Hope and Memory—may be the obvious conditions of life, but like the complications of our relationships, they cheat us of the difficult ecstasy of moment-to-moment consciousness. [22] For Thoreau "the whole duty of life is contained in the question how to respire and aspire both at once" (*W*, VII, 300). He would complain of the hardness of his task—"In all my travels I never came to the abode of the present" (*W*, VIII, 74)—and continually spur himself to new efforts:

> I must live above all in the present. (*Ibid.*, 138)

> My life as essentially belongs to the present as that of a willow tree in the spring. Now, now, its catkins expand, its yellow bark shines, its sap flows; now or never must you make whistles of it. (*W*, IX, 232)

Both for bodily and mental health, court the present. (*W*, X, 432)

Nothing must be postponed. Take time by the forelock. Now or never! You must live in the present, launch yourself on every wave, find your eternity in each moment. Fools stand on their island opportunities and look toward another land. There is no other land; there is no other life but this, or the like of this. (*W*, XVIII, 159)

But once having reached it, he could describe "the abode of the present" as having all the serenity of a perfect geometric figure: "That which presents itself to us this moment occupies the whole of the present and rests on the very topmost point of the sphere, under the zenith" (*W*, XX, 119). Indeed, it was precisely to recommend this abode to those unfamiliar with it that he wrote *Walden*:

I do not mean to prescribe rules to . . . those who find their encouragement and inspiration in precisely the present condition of things, and cherish it with the fondness and enthusiasm of lovers,—and, to some extent, I reckon myself in this number. . . . In any weather, at any hour of the day or night, I have been anxious to improve the nick of time, and notch it on my stick too; to stand on the meeting of two eternities, the past and future, which is precisely the present moment; to toe that line. (*W*, II, 17–18)

"We should be blessed," he suggests in that book, "if we lived in the present always" (*Ibid.*, 346). For it is exactly in the present moment that Thoreau discovers his religious experience:

God himself culminates in the present moment, and will never be more divine in the lapse of all the ages. And we are enabled to apprehend at all what is sublime and noble only by the perpetual instilling and drenching of the reality that surrounds us. (*Ibid.*, 107–8)

Emerson too, in his "Divinity School Address," tells us "that God is, not was" (*C*, I, 144). But, as ever, the God of Emerson and the God of Thoreau are not the same. Emerson's God, reached only through the power of the exalted *Vernunft-Allgemeinheit* (Reason-Universality), is the moral sentiment —Hegel's "Concrete Universal." The God of Thoreau, however, dependent entirely on the lowly *Verstandes-Allgemeinheit* (Understanding-Universality), is simply the apotheosis of what, for Hegel, is a world of nonexistent particulars.

IV

Thoreau's preparation for his moments of mystical revelation, as we have already noticed, consisted entirely of a total immersion of his senses in the natural world. In religious or perhaps psychological terms, these preparatory acts seem sometimes to resemble a species of purification rite. There is an inordinate amount of bathing described in his journal, and it often sounds particularly significant:

> I bathe me in the river. I lie down where it is shallow, amid the weeds over its sandy bottom; but it seems shrunken and parched; I find it difficult to get *wet* through. I would fain be the channel of a mountain brook. I bathe, and in a few hours I bathe again, not remembering that I was wetted before. (*W*, VIII, 335)

Elsewhere he makes explicit the function of his bathing: "I am made more vigorous by my bath, am more *continent* of thought" (*Ibid.*, 435). But the bath not only helps him to contain his vigor; it also cleanses: "Open all your pores and bathe in all the tides of Nature, in all her streams and oceans, at all seasons. Miasma and infection are from within, not without" (*W*, XI, 394). Yet, whatever need Thoreau may have felt to purify himself certainly merges, in his descriptions of bathing, with a sheer physical pleasure in the activity:

I had already bathed in Walden as I passed, but now I forgot that I had been wetted, and wanted to embrace and mingle myself with the water of Flint's Pond this warm afternoon, to get wet inwardly and deeply. (W, VIII, 501)

"Bathing," he wrote on another occasion, "is an undescribed luxury. To feel the wind blow on your body, the water flow on you and lave you, is a rare physical enjoyment this hot day" (W, X, 207). He could even bathe in the breeze when it was still too cold for the pond: "I love to sit in the wind on this hill and be blown on. We bathe thus first in air; then, when the air has warmed it, in water" (W, XI, 159). And, finally, in the heat of full summer he would immerse himself completely:

What a luxury to bathe now! It is gloriously hot,—the first of this weather. I cannot get wet enough. I must let the water soak into me. When you come out, it is rapidly dried on you or absorbed into your body, and you want to go in again. I begin to inhabit the planet, and see how I may be naturalized at last. (W, XII, 382–83)

The ultimate function of bathing was that it "naturalized" him, which was always the necessary preparation for his being "spiritualized." This is perhaps the point of an anecdote which he relates in *Walden:*

As I walked on the railroad causeway, I used to wonder at the halo of light around my shadow, and would fain fancy myself one of the elect. One who visited me declared that the shadows of some Irishmen before him had no halo about them, that it was only natives that were so distinguished. (W, II, 224)

Apart from Thoreau's Yankee sense of humor (no Irishman could possibly be one of New England's "visible elect"!), the moral of the story seems to be that—unlike Benvenuto Cellini (a Catholic, like the Irishmen), for whom a similar experience was "basis enough for superstition"—Thoreau has been "so distinguished" for natural, rather than supernatural, reasons. Only someone who is "native to the universe" (*W*, VIII, 46) can have a truly religious experience. Thus in his journal Thoreau describes his eating of berries as if it were the preparation for a spiritual vocation in nature: "We pluck and eat in remembrance of Her. It is a sacrament, a communion" (*W*, XI, 331).

If we may allow ourselves to borrow St. Bernard's triadic scheme for the mystical apotheosis of the Reason, it is entirely possible to describe Thoreau's religious quest similarly, in terms of three levels of experience. To be sure, the categories will hardly stay put rigidly, and there is liable to be some haziness in the mid-range; but Thoreau himself seems clearly to delineate three stages of natural experience: "joy," "ecstasy," and what we might call the *epiphanic moment*. It was, it seems, mainly for the sake of this latter experience that Thoreau spent so many lonely days tramping in the woods; and it was the memory of these illuminated moments that carried him through the rigors of each winter, as he relates in one of his best poems, "Winter Memories":

> Within the circuit of this plodding life,
> There enter moments of an azure hue,
> Untarnished fair as is the violet
> Or anemone, when the spring strews them
> By some meandering rivulet, which make
> The best philosophy untrue that aims
> But to console man for his grievances.
> I have remembered, when the winter came,
> High in my chamber in the frosty nights,
> When in the still light of the cheerful moon,
> On every twig and rail and jutting spout,
> The icy spears were adding to their length
> Against the arrows of the coming sun,
> How in the shimmering noon of summer past

Some unrecorded beam slanted across
The upland pastures where the Johnswort grew . . .
(W, V, 103)

Once again, Emerson misinterpreted when he wrote of Thoreau that "he knew the worth of the Imagination for the
uplifting and consolation of human life, and liked to throw
every thought into a symbol" (C, X, 475). Thoreau's precious
moment has no symbolic reference; moreover, he disdains
consolation and simply waits patiently for the repetition of his
experience, as the closing lines of the poem make clear: "So by
God's cheap economy made rich/To go upon my winter's task
again." He can bear the hard New England winter because
spring, and more "moments of an azure hue," are not far
behind.

"Surely joy is the condition of life" (W, V, 106), he wrote
in "The Natural History of Massachusetts" (where the poem
discussed above also appears). What makes him condemn the
"lives of quiet desperation" which most men lead is simply that
they are joyless; and he advocates a return to nature because,
for him, the natural world is the original source of joy:

> When I took up a fragment of a walnut-shell this morning, I
> saw by its very grain and composition, its form and color, etc.,
> that it was made for happiness. The most brutish and inani-
> mate objects that are made suggest an everlasting and thor-
> ough satisfaction; they are the homes of content. Wood, earth,
> mould, etc., exist for joy. (W, XV, 206–7)

These apparently brutish objects might leave stolid men un-
moved, but they communicate their satisfaction to Thoreau.
His animal contentment, which he describes in a letter to
Blake as being "a good deal like that of the woodchucks," [23]
often seems no more than a simple sense of physical well-
being: "It is a bright, clear, warm November day. I feel
blessed. I love my life. I warm toward all nature" (W, IX, 86).

Yet he admits that the precise source of his joy is obscure, as when he describes his looking into a grove of pine trees: "I do not know exactly what it was that attracted my eye. I experienced a transient gladness, at any rate, at something which I saw" (*Ibid.*, 131). He is baffled by his own sentiments: "Why should it be so pleasing to look into a thick pine wood where the sunlight streams in and gilds it?" (*Ibid.*, 142). Nevertheless, he is willing to attribute his joy merely to the perfection of the natural world: "Methinks I am in better spirits and physical health now that melons are ripe. . . . The clouds do not entirely disperse, but, since it is decidedly fair and serene, I am contented" (*W*, X, 332). And it is exactly this serene acceptance of his natural environment that constitutes Thoreau's inspirational message to his disciple H. G. O. Blake:

> I am grateful for what I am & have. My thanksgiving is perpetual. It is surprising how contented one can be with nothing definite—only a sense of existance [*sic*]. Well anything for variety. I am ready to try this for the next 1000 years, & exhaust it. How sweet to think of! My extremities well charred, and my intellectual part too, so that there is no danger of worm or rot for a long while. My breath is sweet to me. O how I laugh when I think of my vague indefinite riches. No run on my bank can drain it—for my wealth is not possession but enjoyment.[24]

Yet, of course, since Thoreau's enjoyment was always dependent to a large extent on his physical vitality, the possibility of "drain" was a very real one. He would admit, in fact, in his journal, to being a "torn fragment"; but he could add: ". . . not the less cheerfully we expand in a moist day and assume unexpected colors. We want not completeness but intensity of life" (*W*, XV, 378). And he would insist that we should "measure our lives by our joys. We have lived, not in proportion to the number of years that we have spent on the earth, but in proportion as we have enjoyed" (*W*, XIX, 159).

Not only was joy a sufficient end in itself; it could be a sign that something else was to follow: "No man ever makes a discovery, ever . . . an observation of the least importance, but he is advertised of the fact by a joy that surprises him" (*W*, X, 292). Thoreau's joy appears also to have been a kind of thanks-offering to the machinery of nature which prepared him for further experience: "I love and celebrate nature, even in detail, merely because I love the scenery of these interviews and translations" (*W*, XV, 209–10). Who or what, we may ask, was being "translated," if not Thoreau himself?

In a letter to Blake dated May 21, 1856, Thoreau insisted that it was the high importance of "translation" that made for his lack of sociability, not an intrinsic dislike of people:

> As for the dispute about solitude & society any comparison is impertinent. It is an idling down on the plain at the base of a mountain instead of climbing steadily to its top. Of course you will be glad of all the society you can get to go up with. Will you go to glory with me? is the burden of the song. I love society so much that I swallowed it all at a gulp—i.e. all that came in my way. It is not that we love to be alone, but that we love to soar, and when we do soar, the company grows thinner & thinner till there is none at all. It is either the Tribune on the plain, a sermon on the mount, or a very private *extacy* still higher up.[25]

Of these three kinds of activity—plebeian affairs, Transcendentalism of the verbal-ethical sort, and "very private *extacy*"—Thoreau declares himself thoroughly committed to the last, an ecstasy which (unlike the shared rapture that John Donne describes in "The Ecstasy") is for him a solitary occupation. He had confided his preference to his journal in 1851:

> My desire for knowledge is intermittent; but my desire to commune with the spirit of the universe, to be intoxicated even with the fumes, call it, of that divine nectar, to bear my

head through atmospheres and over heights unknown to my feet, is perennial and constant. (*W*, VIII, 150–51)

Thoreau tried to give a description of this experience—by his own admission, a constant preoccupation—to the largest audience he ever reached, the readers of *Walden,* but those who have studied the journal can only pronounce this "revery" a considerably toned-down public exhibition of yoga:

> Sometimes, in a summer morning, having taken my accustomed bath, I sat in my sunny doorway from sunrise till noon, rapt in a revery, amidst the pines and hickories and sumachs, in undisturbed solitude and stillness, while the birds sang around or flitted noiseless through the house, until by the sun falling in at my west window, or the noise of some traveller's wagon on the distant highway, I was reminded of the lapse of time. I grew in those seasons like corn in the night, and they were far better than any work of the hands would have been. They were not time subtracted from my life, but so much over and above my usual allowance. (*W*, II, 123–24)

Among other things, the measure of Thoreau's concession to his audience here is the use of an economic metaphor at the close of the description—that economic metaphor which constitutes the one pervasive deception in *Walden,* for, as he was to say of nature in a journal entry for 1859, "her motive is not economy but satisfaction" (*W*, XVIII, 96). Moreover, Thoreau's self-parody in his description of the genesis of a "budding ecstasy" later in the book makes it plain that he thought it unwise to bare his soul completely in *Walden.* In this passage, he has just been disturbed by the visit of a "Poet" (presumably Ellery Channing):

> *Hermit alone.* Let me see; where was I? Methinks I was nearly in this frame of mind; the world lay about this angle. Shall I go to heaven or a-fishing? If I should soon bring this meditation to an end, would another so sweet occasion be likely to

offer? I was as near being resolved into the essence of things as ever I was in my life. I fear my thoughts will not come back to me. If it would do any good, I would whistle for them. When they make us an offer, is it wise to say, We will think of it? My thoughts have left no track, and I cannot find the path again. What was it that I was thinking of? It was a very hazy day. I will just try these three sentences of Confut-see; they may fetch that state about again. I know not whether it was the dumps or a budding ecstasy. (*W*, II, 248–49)

In the journal Thoreau never seems to have trouble distinguishing between the "dumps" and a "budding ecstasy." Furthermore, the latter state is rarely described as being inducible through reading—of Confucius or anybody else. It is shown, rather, to be the result of natural experience, particularly in connection with the sun, as in this "introduction" to an ecstasy in the journal for 1841:

In the sunshine and the crowing of cocks I feel an illimitable holiness, which makes me bless God and myself. The warm sun casts his incessant gift at my feet as I walk along, unfolding his yellow worlds. (*W*, VII, 202)

The *rondo estatico* which follows completes the experience:

The eaves are running on the south side of the house; the titmouse lisps in the poplar; the bells are ringing for church; while the sun presides over all and makes his simple warmth more obvious than all else. What shall I do with this hour, so like time and yet so fit for eternity? . . . I lie out indistinct as a heath at noonday. I am evaporating and ascending into the sun. (*Ibid.*, 203–4)

This kind of "translation" could also be effected by sound, to the divine powers of which Thoreau considered himself particularly sensitive. And in the privacy of his journal he could describe the experience with considerably less inhibition than the public nature of *Walden* imposed:

The strains of the aeolian harp and of the wood thrush . . . lift us up in spite of ourselves. They intoxicate, they charm us. Where was that strain mixed into which this world was dropped but as a lump of sugar to sweeten the draught? I would be drunk, drunk, drunk, dead drunk to this world with it forever. He that hath ears, let him hear. The contact of sound with a human ear whose hearing is pure and unimpaired is coincident with an ecstasy. . . . It, as it were, takes me out of my body and gives me the freedom of all bodies and all nature. I leave my body in a trance and accompany the zephyr and the fragrance. (*W*, XII, 39–40)

The reader of Thoreau with no sympathy for mystic states may be inclined to write off his descriptions of his ecstasies as simply hyperbole, or perhaps even affectation; but there is a good deal of evidence to show that neither explanation will suffice, that Thoreau was writing of something he knew. In the year of the passage quoted above (1853), he entered a paragraph of apparently etymological import in his journal:

True words are those, as Trench says,—transport, rapture, ravishment, ecstasy. These are the words I want. This is the effect of music. I am rapt away by it, out of myself. These are truly poetical words. I am inspired, elevated, expanded. I am on the mount.[26]

It might at first seem curious that Thoreau, with all his insistence on the concrete and the factual, would approve of these abstract terms. One can only conclude that they must have signified some real experience to him. And, indeed, we find that the statement "I am on the mount" is at once one of Thoreau's favorite metaphors for his ecstatic moments and a literal description of one of the ways in which ecstasy could be attained.

"I am not taken up," Thoreau wrote in 1840, "like Moses, upon a mountain to learn the law, but lifted up in my seat here, in the warm sunshine and genial light" (*W*, VII, 158). His refusal here to be identified with Moses upon Sinai was not to preclude, as we shall see, his associating himself with Moses upon Pisgah. Indeed, that was the very distinction he was making: unlike the other Transcendentalists, his concern was ecstasy—and ecstatic illumination—rather than ethics. Occasionally, to be sure, he could present the two possibilities without explicitly choosing:

> Sometimes I come out suddenly upon a high plain, which seems to be the upper level and true surface of the earth, and by its very baldness aspires and lies up nearer to the stars,—a place where a decalogue might be let down or a saint translated. (*Ibid.*, 186)

One assumes, knowing his attitude toward receiving the decalogue and his desire for "translation," that it was really the latter he awaited. But he would claim to be happy to receive whatever came his way:

> I only ask a clean seat. I will build my lodge on the southern slope of some hill, and take there the life the gods send me. Will it not be employment enough to accept gratefully all that is yielded me between sun and sun? (*Ibid.*, 244)

What the gods actually yielded Thoreau, however, was not very palpable, for of the "many a day spent on the hilltops waiting for the sky to fall, that I might catch something," he could only report that he "never caught much, only a little, manna-wise, that would dissolve again in the sun" (*Ibid.*, 435). But this was hardly important; he expected nothing palpable: "A greater baldness my life seeks, as the crest of some bare hill, which towns and cities do not afford. I want a directer relation with the sun" (*Ibid.*, 248). This latter-day follower of Apollo, relieved from time to time of the necessity of slaving for his Admetus, wanted only to re-establish contact with his master and, if not to receive an oracle, at least to be seized with sibylline rapture. Finally, of course, being "on the mount" was for Thoreau not simply a question of sublime sun-bathing but a metaphor for the ecstasy leading to an illuminated moment: "There is elevation in every hour," and "we have only to stand on the eminence of the hour, and look out thence into the empyrean" (*Ibid.*, 214). To be sure, all hours are not equally eminent; the coincidence of an ecstasy and a vision is rare, and one's whole life must be devoted to awaiting the occasion:

> If by patience, if by watching, I can secure one new ray of light, can feel myself elevated for an instant upon Pisgah, the world which was dead prose to me becoming living and divine, shall I not watch ever? Shall I not be a watchman henceforth? If by watching a whole year on the city's walls I may obtain a communication from heaven, shall I not do well to shut up my shop and turn a watchman? (*W*, VIII, 471)

Thoreau's profession was that of watchman, and he had to be always on the alert for the feeling of elevation and a "new ray of light." The job was arduous and unending:

> Not only narrow but rough is the way that leadeth to life everlasting. Our experience does not wear upon us. It is seen to be fabulous or symbolical, and the future is worth expecting. Encouraged, I set out once more to climb the mountain of the earth, for my steps are symbolical steps, and in all my walking I have not reached the top of the earth yet. (*W*, XI, 35)

The perfect Pisgah-sight, equivalent for Thoreau to the "abode of the present" (*W*, VIII, 74), was a moment of total ecstasy and illumination, and it was worth attending. One might say that his dedication to the job approximated, *mutatis mutandis*, that of the great mystic philosopher Plotinus. Indeed, in his journal for 1840 Thoreau made the following notation:

> Plotinus aimed at ἐπαφήν, and παρουσίαν ἐπιστήμης κρείττονα and τὸ ἑαυτὸν κέντρον τῷ οἷον πάντων κέντρῳ συνάπτειν. (*W*, VII, 139)

Plotinus aimed at "contact" (or "apprehension") and the "greater presence of knowledge," and at "uniting his own center with the center of all things." It would seem that Thoreau decided early to make this his own program. Being "on the mount" was a way of describing that "contact" with the One of Plotinus which led to the "greater presence of knowledge." Like Plotinus, what Thoreau brought back from his experience of union with the center of all things was teasingly ineffable.

The union that Plotinus advocated was one involving a man's total being: the coincidence of ecstatic feeling with perfect vision. This was Thoreau's goal as a naturalist—a difficult goal and not one that he could depend on attaining always. It remained his principal occupation, as he suggested in the following letter to Blake in 1857, five years before his death:

> With regard to essentials, I have never had occasion to change my mind. The aspect of the world varies from year to year, as the landscape is differently clothed, but I find that the *truth* is still *true,* and I never regret any emphasis which it may have inspired. Ktaadn [Mt. Katahdin] is there still, but much more surely my old conviction is there, resting with more than mountain breadth and weight on the world, the source still of fertilizing streams, and affording glorious views from its summit, if I can get up to it again.[27]

As always, the natural world is the source of Thoreau's intense delight, which finds its perfect end in the moment of illumination—the final stage in Thoreau's mystic quest, when the heat of ecstasy has been transformed totally into light. This is certainly what he means here by the somewhat curious use of "emphasis." The world is still to be depended upon, and he does not regret what it has always inspired, an "emphasis"— literally, an appearance—exactly equivalent in its root meaning to "epiphany." This vision it was that Thoreau always and finally aimed for, as he confessed to Blake in 1848: "My only integral experience is in my vision. I see, perchance, with more integrity than I feel." [28]

To judge by his writings, Thoreau had a fair amount of success in attaining this integral and integrative experience. In his journal for 1841, for instance, he relates how noteworthy an event a moment of illumination could be for him:

> Whole weeks or months of my summer life slide away in thin volumes like mist or smoke, till at length some warm morning, perchance, I see a sheet of mist blown down the brook to the swamp, its shadow flitting across the fields, which have caught a new significance from that accident; and as that vapor is raised above the earth, so shall the next weeks be elevated above the plane of the actual . . . (*W*, VII, 300–1)

That "new significance"—accidental, and a part of the phenomenal world—transforms the actual in a major way, as Thoreau was to note the following year:

> All sights and sounds are seen and heard both in time and eternity. And when the eternity of any sight or sound strikes the eye or ear, they are intoxicated with delight. Sometimes, as through a dim haze, we see objects in their eternal relations. (*Ibid.*, 359)

The delight, then, of seeing things under the aspect of eternity elevates the ordinary events of Thoreau's life. Moreover, "we are never so visionary as to be prepared for what the next hour may bring forth" (*W*, IV, 301). The shift in vision may occur at any hour and is sudden: "The change from foulness to serenity is instantaneous. Suddenly an influx of light, though it was late, filled my room" (*W*, VII, 400). Here the illumination takes place in his chamber, but Thoreau's best descriptions of epiphanic moments are of outdoor occurrences. In them there is an almost eerie mingling of exact detail and visionary suggestion:

Some distant angle in the sun where a lofty and dense white pine wood, with mingled gray and green, meets a hill covered with shrub oaks, affects me singularly, reinspiring me with all the dreams of my youth. It is a place far away, yet actual and where we have been. I saw the sun falling on a distant white pine wood whose gray and moss-covered stems were visible amid the green, in an angle where this forest abutted on a hill covered with shrub oaks. It was like looking into dreamland. It is one of the avenues to my future. Certain coincidences like this are accompanied by a certain flash as of hazy lightning, flooding all the world suddenly with a tremulous serene light which it is difficult to see long at a time. (W, VIII, 106-7)

Sometimes his descriptions are actually dramatic:

The pines standing in the ocean of mist, seen from the Cliffs, are trees in every stage of transition from the actual to the imaginary. . . . As you advance, the trees gradually come out of the mist and take form before your eyes. You are reminded of your dreams. Life looks like a dream. You are prepared to see visions. And now, just before sundown, the night wind blows up more mist through the valley, thickening the veil which already hung over the trees, and the gloom of night gathers early and rapidly around. Birds lose their way. (Ibid., 119)

One senses the presence of powers which are on the verge of exposing themselves; but at the crucial moment, the wind stirs, the world is engulfed in darkness, and we are left with a keen sense of loss—loss of the vision, that moment of illumination which was always so highly significant for Thoreau:

I do not know that knowledge amounts to anything more definite than a novel and grand surprise, or a sudden revelation of the insufficiency of all that we had called knowledge before; an indefinite sense of the grandeur and glory of the universe. It is the lighting up of the mist by the sun. (Ibid., 168)

The importance of the epiphanic moment, then, is simply that it constitutes the highest way of knowing—precisely that "greater presence of knowledge" aimed at by Plotinus. But unfortunately this knowledge is ineffable in philosophical or scientific terms: "Your greatest success will be simply to perceive that such things are, and you will have no communication to make to the Royal Society" (*W*, XVIII, 371). Still, Thoreau would find himself perpetually teased and perplexed by his experience:

> If any part of nature excites our pity, it is for ourselves we grieve. . . . We get only transient and partial glimpses of the beauty of the world. . . . Beauty and music are not mere traits and exceptions. They are the rule and character. It is the exception that we see and hear. Then I try to discover what it was in the vision that charmed and translated me. What if we could daguerreotype our thoughts and feelings! for I am surprised and enchanted often by some quality which I cannot detect. I have seen an attribute of another world and condition of things. It is a wonderful fact that I should be affected, and thus deeply and powerfully, more than by aught else in all my experience . . . (*W*, XIV, 44–45)

Thoreau could grieve for himself that his "glimpses of the beauty of the world" were only partial and intermittent, and their nature ineffable. Nevertheless, the wonder was that the glimpses did come and that their arrival made such an enormous difference. The momentary experience might be no more than a vision of sunlight on pine needles, yet Thoreau could exclaim in ecstasy: "At sight of this my spirit is like a lit tree" (*W*, XVI, 305). The supreme value of the epiphanic moment for Thoreau was simply its power to effect a total transformation of his spirit from dejection to exaltation. It was the secret of his Transcendentalism, as he suggested in a letter to Blake in 1853:

I have had but one *spiritual* birth (excuse the word,) and now whether it rains or snows, whether I laugh or cry, fall farther below or approach nearer to my standard, whether Pierce or Scott is elected,—not a new scintillation of light flashes on me, but ever and anon, though with longer intervals, the same surprising & everlastingly new light dawns to me, with only such variations as in the coming of the natural day, with which indeed, it is often coincident.[29]

It was exactly the importance of this ever-new but perennial light, this *real* vision, that Thoreau had tried—somewhat mystifyingly, in the midst of a long series of quotations from the Bhagavad-Gita—to communicate to the readers of *A Week*:

The most glorious fact in my experience is not anything that I have done or may hope to do, but a transient thought, or vision, or dream, which I have had. I would give all the wealth of the world, and all the deeds of all the heroes, for one true vision. (*W*, I, 145–46)

So much for his readers; the conclusion of the paragraph was clearly addressed by Thoreau to himself: "But how can I communicate with the gods, who am a pencil-maker on the earth, and not be insane?" Certainly his Concord neighbors thought him queer enough for racing around the woods to no apparent purpose; now Thoreau stopped to ask himself whether his being an equerry of epiphanies wasn't a rather precarious profession. Nevertheless, they were what he believed in, and his message remained unchanged in *Walden*:

If the day and the night are such that you greet them with joy, and life emits a fragrance like flowers and sweet-scented herbs, is more elastic, more starry, more immortal,—that is your success. All nature is your congratulation, and you have cause momentarily to bless yourself. The greatest gains and values are farthest from being appreciated. We easily come to doubt if they exist. We soon forget them. They are the highest reality. Perhaps the facts most astounding and most real are never communicated by man to man. The true harvest of my daily life is somewhat as intangible and indescribable as the tints of morning or evening. It is a little star-dust caught, a segment of the rainbow which I have clutched. (*W*, II, 239)

Thoreau's statement of his theory is clearly somewhat more "poetic" and less direct here than in *A Week;* and it is perhaps in the earlier work, before his youthful exuberance was tempered by failure, that he truly succeeded in conveying the "*hypaethral* character" (*W*, VIII, 274) of his culminating Transcendental experience—total vision reached in nature through the five senses, a purely sensuous life. In *A Week* Thoreau could shout exultantly:

> I see, smell, taste, hear, feel, that everlasting Something to which we are allied, at once our maker, our abode, our destiny, our very Selves; the one historic truth, the most remarkable fact which can become the distinct and uninvited subject of our thought, the actual glory of the universe . . . (*W*, I, 182)

Thoreau's uniqueness as a Transcendentalist resides in the fact that he attained the end of a Plotinian philosopher—the union of his own center with the center of all things—by purely Lockean means. And since the world was simply not prepared to "go to glory" with him (although he democratically offered everyone a ticket to his "Celestial Railroad" in *A Week* and *Walden*), he had decided early in life that it would be a sufficient career for him to go alone and send back news of what he found.

v

As an American writer, Thoreau was undoubtedly far ahead of his time in building his life and art on a theory of ecstatic and illuminated moments reached through sense experience. Certainly, one can think of no less propitious time and place for such a theory than nineteenth-century America just prior to the Civil War. For, even more than Edgar Allan Poe, who (as everyone knows) died in a Baltimore gutter in 1849, more a victim of obscurity than of alcohol, Thoreau was a *pure* aesthete. In 1847, in response to a questionnaire circulated by the secretary of his graduating class at Harvard (1837), Thoreau wrote rather flippantly: ". . . my steadiest employment, if such it can be called, is to keep myself at the top of my condition, and ready for whatever may turn up in heaven or on earth."[30] For all his desire to shock, he was obviously making an honest statement. Five years before, at the age of twenty-five, he had confessed in his journal what he hoped to do with his life:

> I would fain communicate the wealth of my life to men, would really give them what is most precious in my gift. I would secrete pearls with the shellfish and lay up honey with the bees for them. I will sift the sunbeams for the public good. . . . I wish to communicate those parts of my life which I would gladly live again myself. (*W*, VII, 350)

Thoreau's aims—and their form, that of youthful artistic pretension, purposely assumed—are recognizably those of another age. Had he been born fifty years later, with the generation that came to maturity in the nineties, he would probably have had not only more suitable friends and a more appreciative audience but also a spiritual father, Walter Pater. It is suggestive to consider Thoreau in the context of some of the well-known dicta at the conclusion of Pater's *The Renaissance*:

> *Philosophiren*, says Novalis, *ist dephlegmatisiren, vivificiren*. The service of philosophy, of speculative culture, towards the human spirit, is to rouse, to startle it to a life of constant and eager observation. Every moment some form grows perfect in hand or face; some tone on the hills or the sea is choicer than the rest; some mood of passion or insight or intellectual

excitement is irresistibly real and attractive to us,—for that
moment only. Not the fruit of experience, but experience
itself, is the end. . . . To burn always with this hard, gemlike
flame, to maintain this ecstasy, is success in life. . . . With
this sense of the splendour of our experience and of its awful
brevity, gathering all we are into one desperate effort to see
and touch, we shall hardly have time to make theories about
the things we see and touch. . . . Our one chance lies
in . . . getting as many pulsations as possible into the given
time.[31]

Many of Thoreau's constant concerns are strikingly summarized in this passage of Pater's—the necessity of awakening
ourselves, of remaining keenly aware of our experience in the
world; the poignant sense of process, and the concomitant need
to live passionately and sensuously in each moment as it passes;
and finally, the notion that art has less to do with explaining
and theorizing about our ecstatic moments than simply with
heightening and recording them.

It is this insistence on the importance of momentary experience that marks so many of the aesthetes of the pre-World War
I period as the spiritual children of Pater. Bernard Berenson,
for instance, suggests the notion well when he writes of
himself: "Moments of greatest happiness . . . were moments
when I lost myself all but completely in some instant of perfect
harmony." [32] Even more importantly, George Santayana con-
structed his whole mature philosophy on a theory—the theory
of "essences"—which, on its imaginative side, can certainly be
termed Paterish. For Santayana, the business of a spiritual (or
artistic) life is the experiencing of the "ultimate in the immediate," the realization of an "essence"—a fugitive but perfect
moment of illumination.[33] This realization is necessarily predicated on sense experience in the world of existence, but the
spiritual man is freed from the imputation of sensualism
because his desire for the world is *pure*: he seeks momentary

harmonies, not objects of possession. Moreover, this realization
has nothing necessarily to do with the true cosmology of the
universe: "Mortal spirits, the spirit in animals, cannot possibly
survey pure Being in its infinity; but in so far as they free
themselves from false respect for the objects of animal faith
and animal passion, they may behold some finite being in its
purity." [34]

Santayana's criticism of Emerson is based precisely on the
fact that, in Santayana's judgment, Emerson was not concerned with "some finite being in its purity"—the object, for
Santayana, of a truly spiritual life—nor even (as Emerson
himself thought) with "pure Being in its infinity," but rather
with the poetic rendering of an inherited ethical system:

> . . . he was not an independent philosopher, in spite of his
> belief in independence. He inherited the problems and the
> preoccupations of the theology from which he started, being in
> this respect like the German idealists, who, with all their
> pretence of absolute metaphysics, were in reality only giving
> elusive and abstract forms to traditional theology. Emerson,
> too, was not primarily a philosopher, but a Puritan mystic with
> a poetic fancy and a gift for observation and epigram, and he
> saw in the laws of Nature, idealised by his imagination, only a
> more intelligible form of the divinity he had always recognised
> and adored. His was not a philosophy passing into a religion,
> but a religion expressing itself as a philosophy and veiled, as at
> its setting it descended the heavens, in various tints of poetry
> and science.[35]

Unfortunately, there is no evidence that Santayana ever read
anything of Thoreau's and therefore no way of knowing what
he might have thought of Thoreau's experiments in beholding
"some finite being in its purity." Santayana would undoubtedly
have been surprised to find adumbrations of his own ideas in
nineteenth-century American writing; when he sought confirmation of his theory of "essential moments" in contemporary

opinion, he turned to Europe. In philosophy he found the "Pure Phenomenology" of Edmund Husserl, with whom he felt in substantial agreement and whose ideas pleased him, except for Husserl's Kantian over-concern with the operations of the mind itself. "A naturalist," Santayana said in firm demurral, "must . . . look for the genesis and meaning of immediate experience in the material and animal world, where a malicious transcendentalism, one that isolates mind in mind, cannot consistently look for them." [36] Thoreau's view, one feels, would ultimately have pleased Santayana more than Husserl's.

Among contemporary imaginative writers, Santayana found in Proust a more than satisfactory corroboration of his theory. Santayana was pleased to discover what he considered to be Proust's realization that "an essence is simply the recognisable character of any object or feeling, all of it that can actually be possessed in sensation or recovered in memory, or transcribed in art, or conveyed to another mind," and that "all that was intrinsically real in past time is accordingly recoverable." Proust's discovery of this, Santayana avers, led him to become the "tireless husbandman of memory"—in Proust's own words (which Santayana quotes at length): "And so I was decided to consecrate myself to this study of the essence of things, to establish its true nature." [37]

It is perhaps surprising that this consecration to the study of cherished moments, which Santayana admired in Proust, he failed to see in the writings of James Joyce. In a letter written in 1931, Santayana claimed that Proust's introduction of "infinite details . . . had two qualities not found . . . in Joyce": "a *poetic* quality," and the fact that in Proust "the details themselves are beautiful or interesting, they are selected by an *active intellect*." [38] This seems a curious pronouncement, but it is even more curious that Santayana failed to notice Joyce's theory of "epiphanies," which has a strong affinity to his own theory of "essences." As outlined by Richard Ellmann, Joyce believed that "the epiphany was the sudden 'revelation of the whatness of a thing,' the moment in which 'the soul of the commonest object . . . seems to us radiant.' The artist, he felt, was charged with such revelations, and must look for them not among gods but among men, in casual, unostentatious, even unpleasant moments." [39] Harry Levin's summary of Joyce's theory is even more suggestive:

> An epiphany is a spiritual manifestation. . . . There are such moments in store for all of us, Joyce believed, if we but discern them. Sometimes, amid the most encumbered circumstances, it suddenly happens that the veil is lifted, the burthen of the mystery laid bare, and the ultimate secret of things made manifest. Such a sudden intimation was experienced by Marcel Proust, when he had dipped a bit of *madeleine* into a cup of linden tea. Such a momentary vision, perhaps too intimate to be included in the final version of the *Portrait of the Artist,* had once come to Stephen Dedalus, passing through Eccles Street, before "one of those brown brick houses which seem the very incarnation of Irish paralysis." It now seemed to him that the task of the man of letters was to record these delicate and evanescent states of mind, to become a collector of epiphanies. Walking along the beach, in *Ulysses,* he muses upon his own collection, and his youthful resolve to leave copies to all the libraries of the world, including Alexandria.[40]

Here—with Joyce's gently ironic description of the young aesthete, Stephen Dedalus, who aspires only to be a "collector of epiphanies"—the generation fathered by Pater inadvertently suggests its prototype in Thoreau (much admired, we may note in passing, by Proust and Yeats), who, like the young Stephen, saw himself as a collector of epiphanic moments.

If we define the artist, along with Henry James, as "one of the people on whom nothing is lost," [41] Thoreau was eminently conscious of his job. "May I gird myself to be a hunter of the beautiful," he exclaimed in 1852, "that naught escape me! . . . I am eager to report the glory of the universe; may I be worthy to do it" (*W*, IX, 351). For Thoreau the artistic life demanded two things: the ability to live to the fullest, and the power to report the results. In a full and intense life, moments of illumination were simply the necessary concomitant of true pulsations and passionate attitudes:

> The scenery, when it is truly seen, reacts on the life of the seer. How to live. How to get the most life. As if you were to teach the young hunter how to entrap his game. How to extract its honey from the flower of the world. That is my every-day business. . . . The art of spending a day. If it is possible that we may be addressed, it behooves us to be attentive. If by watching all day and all night I may detect some trace of the Ineffable, then will it not be worth the while to watch? (*W*, VIII, 470–71)

For Thoreau, not only was it worth the while to watch; it was an ancient and honorable profession. He obviously believed, with Henry James, in "the perfect dependence of the 'moral' sense of a work of art on the amount of felt life concerned in producing it." [42] Thus Thoreau attacked the English author Hugh Miller for suggesting that there was a "want of harmony between 'the perception and love of the beautiful' and a delicate moral sense" (*W*, IX, 30–31). For Thoreau morality in art resided not in the theme, but in the truth of the artist's materials and methods. It galled him to realize that he was thought to be vaguely disreputable by his neighbors—a tinkerer with trifles:

> My work is writing, and I do not hesitate, though I know that no subject is too trivial for me, tried by ordinary standards; for, ye fools, the theme is nothing, the life is everything. All that interests the reader is the depth and intensity of the life excited. (*W*, XV, 121)

Moments of illumination were "moral" moments in that they were moments of "felt life." This it was that Thoreau aimed at, and he was confident that, at least ultimately, only art reared on such a conviction would succeed:

> If the writer would interest readers, he must report so much life, using a certain satisfaction always as a *point d'appui.* However mean and limited, it must be a genuine and contented life that he speaks out of. They must have the essence or oil of himself, tried out of the fat of his experience and joy. (*Ibid.,* 195)

Despite his declaration of moral independence, however, Thoreau was far from lacking the desire to succeed. To be sure, in criticizing Hugh Miller (in 1851) he could write: "He [Miller] speaks of his work becoming all in all to the worker, his rising above the dread of criticism and the appetite of praise, as if these were the very rare exceptions in a great artist's life, and not the very definition of it" (*W*, IX, 31). Here again, in Thoreau's defensive pose, we are reminded of the later nineteenth century and the "enigma of manner" with which, as self-protection, Joyce endowed his Stephen Hero.[43] Nevertheless, Thoreau hoped to win the title of benefactor from his townsmen if he could "conquer some realms from the night . . . show them that there is some beauty awake while they are asleep . . . add to the domains of poetry . . . report to the gazettes anything transpiring in our midst worthy of man's attention" (*W*, VIII, 478–79).

Thoreau's artist-hero was not just the man who experiences epiphanies but the one who collects and reshapes them: "He is the man truly—courageous, wise, ingenious—who can use his thoughts and ecstasies as the material of fair and durable creations" (*W*, XVI, 404). Thoreau's journal (the only gazette to which he reported, and one—as he related sadly in *Walden*—"of no very wide circulation" [*W*, II, 19]) was his attempt to collect and use his ecstasies: "My Journal should be the record of my love. I would write in it only of the things I love, my affection for any aspect of the world" (*W*, VIII, 101). His journal was the living repository of his cherished moments: "It is a record of the mellow and ripe moments that I would keep. I would not preserve the husk of life, but the kernel" (*W*, IX, 150). Thoreau himself suggests the difference between his journal and Emerson's: "A journal is a record of experiences and growth, not a preserve of things well done or said" (*W*, XIV, 134).

Unlike Emerson's journal, which was the "savings bank" where Emerson deposited his thoughts and whence he drew his essays, Thoreau's journal is a record of his life and art in the making, and is itself his greatest work. But, unfortunately for those readers who demand form from an artist, it is no more than this: "A journal, a book that shall contain a record of all your joy, your ecstasy" (*W*, X, 223). Thus Henry James could observe shrewdly of Thoreau that although he had genius in abundance, he lacked talent: "He was imperfect, unfinished, inartistic." [44] We may, however, boggle at James's final adjective; lack of significant form has become a familiar characteristic of much art in our own time, the very symbol of our fragmented world view. Nor was Thoreau unaware of his own nature. In 1857 he admitted his lack of "completeness and roundness" by calling himself "a torn fragment" (*W*, XV, 378).

Years before, at the age of twenty-three, he had noted the character of his journal: "It is always a chance scrawl, and commemorates some accident" (*W*, VII, 207). This may not describe Thoreau's method of composition, but it certainly indicates the intent of his journal: God's accidents (to rephrase Sophia Hawthorne's sentence) are man's epiphanies. Thoreau remained, like Joyce's artist as a young man, a collector of epiphanic moments; and his masterpiece, the journal, is a massive collection of these eternal moments snatched ecstatically from the indifferent jaws of time. "I find in my Journal," he wrote in 1855, "that the most important events in my life, if recorded at all, are not dated" (*W*, XIV, 64).

VI

"I live in the perpetual verdure of the globe. I die in the annual decay of nature" (*W*, VII, 324). In this journal entry for 1842, Thoreau set down the quintessence of *Walden*, that triumphant theme of death and rebirth which has made the book so congenial to modern criticism. Thoreau's victory, however, was by no means an easy one and perhaps finally not even so complete as the structure of *Walden* would suggest. The difficulty was that each year Thoreau found himself living a little less in the perpetual verdure of the globe and dying a little more in its annual decay. The loss of youth was a serious problem for him, much more so than for Emerson, who, in the New England tradition, early renounced the passional life and prepared himself for a career of more or less abstract speculation.

"I am past thirty," Matthew Arnold wrote to his friend Clough in 1853, "and three parts iced over." [45] At about the same time Thoreau was beginning to have similar notions, but it was not, one feels, the simple fact of turning thirty (which occurred in 1847) that did the trick for him. Had his first publishing venture brought him any success, it is entirely possible that he could have reconciled himself to a life spent more indoors than he was used to. But the total failure of *A Week* to attract any attention after its publication in 1849 drove Thoreau, with a vengeance, back on himself and his life in nature. What he found, among other things, were some of his first intimations of mortality in the diminished keenness of his senses. At first he tried to argue himself out of the difficulty by an increased insistence on present experience, but there is a perhaps unconscious equivocation in his own argument, as in the following journal entry for June 1850:

> My imagination, my love and reverence and admiration, my sense of the miraculous, is not so excited by any event as by the remembrance of my youth. Men talk about Bible miracles because there is no miracle in their lives. Cease to gnaw that crust. There is ripe fruit over your head. (*W*, VIII, 33)

Thoreau's exhortation seems a curious non sequitur in this context, for the miracle which he opposes to the defunct "Bible miracles" is his youth, itself a past event. By the following June, his barely submerged nostalgia has risen fully to consciousness: "Ah, that life that I have known! How hard it is to remember what is most memorable! . . . I can sometimes recall to mind the quality, the immortality, of my youthful life, but in memory is the only relation to it" (*Ibid.*, 237–38). And one month later he expatiated on the problem in his journal, revealing clearly the crux of his difficulty—the dulling of the senses with increasing age:

> I think that no experience which I have to-day comes up to, or is comparable with, the experiences of my boyhood. . . . My life was ecstasy. In youth, before I lost any of my senses, I can remember that I was all alive, and inhabited my body with inexpressible satisfaction; both its weariness and its refreshment were sweet to me. This earth was the most glorious musical instrument, and I was audience to its strains. To have such sweet impressions made on us, such ecstasies begotten of the breezes! I can remember how I was astonished. I said to myself,—I said to others,—"There comes into my mind such an indescribable, infinite, all-absorbing, divine, heavenly pleasure, a sense of elevation and expansion, and [I] have had nought to do with it. I perceive that I am dealt with by superior powers. This is a pleasure, a joy, an existence which I

have not procured myself. I speak as a witness on the stand, and tell what I have perceived." . . . I was daily intoxicated. (*Ibid.*, 306–7)

To be sure, there was a good deal of intoxication still to be found in his daily experience, but henceforth in the journal his lament for his lost youth becomes a predictable item: "Ah, those youthful days! are they never to return?" (*W*, XI, 75). In the winter especially, when nature offered little to his senses, he could feel his personal loss—the decline of his powers—most keenly:

As I climbed the Cliff, I paused in the sun and sat on a dry rock, dreaming. I thought of those summery hours when time is tinged with eternity—runs into it and becomes of one stuff with it. How much—how, perhaps, all—that is best in our experience in middle life may be resolved into the memory of our youth! I remember how I expanded. If the genius visits me now I am not quite taken off my feet, but I remember how this experience is like, but less than, that I had long since. (*W*, X, 460)

Thoreau was simply realizing that what he called "my vacation, my season of growth and expansion, a prolonged youth" (*W*, XIII, 46) was of finite duration; and since he had built his art on a theory of acute sense experience—in effect, a theory of perpetual youth—the realization was a painful one. On February 6, 1857, as the apparently inconsequent conclusion to a long series of natural observations, he inscribed the following paragraph in his journal:

Winckelmann says in his "History of Ancient Art," vol. i, page 95: "I am now past forty, and therefore at an age when one can no longer sport freely with life. I perceive, also, that a certain delicate spirit begins to evaporate, with which I raised myself, by powerful soarings, to the contemplation of the beautiful." (*W*, XV, 242–43)

This was five months before Thoreau's fortieth birthday, and he quotes the passage without comment.

As a protective stratagem against what he considered his increasing insensibility, Thoreau would occasionally attempt to project his difficulty beyond himself into the external world. "We soon get through with Nature," he wrote in 1854. "She excites an expectation which she cannot satisfy" (*W*, XII, 293). When he felt himself to be still in possession of his youth, however, he had no such complaints to make about nature. Indeed, in 1850 he had taken the blame squarely on his own shoulders: "After the era of youth is passed, the knowledge of ourselves is an alloy that spoils our satisfactions" (*W*, VIII, 77). What he really seems to be complaining about in his 1854 comment is simply that his observations of the external world have confirmed the terrible truth which the decline of his powers of sensation embodied: the threat of personal extinction. If the expectation that Thoreau wanted nature to satisfy was that of perpetual rebirth and the triumph of life—his "infinite expectation of the dawn" (*W*, II, 100)—he was bound to be disappointed, as he discovered in 1851:

> Is not disease the rule of existence? There is not a lily pad floating on the river but has been riddled by insects. Almost every shrub and tree has its gall, oftentimes esteemed its chief ornament and hardly to be distinguished from the fruit. If misery loves company, misery has company enough. Now, at midsummer, find me a perfect leaf or fruit. (*W*, VIII, 440)

Of course, he could attempt to elude what was before his eyes by turning the "gall" into a "fruit" (here is an instance of the trick of paradox that so irked Emerson) or simply by finding beauty in decay: "Decay and disease are often beautiful, like the pearly tear of the shellfish and the hectic glow of consumption" (*W*, X, 91). The device, however, is somewhat less than convincing; indeed, Thoreau is never very convincing when he tries to talk his way out of death, especially when he turns it into a joke through a species of *Galgenhumor*.[46] In his journal, however, when he forces himself to consider the matter seriously, he invariably does so with a very un-Thoreauvian gravity of manner.

Indeed, in the entries dealing with death he often seems to lose control of his prose and to begin ranting in a painful fashion. This is true of the journal passages written after his attempt to find the remains of Margaret Fuller on Fire Island in the summer of 1850, as it is of the ones inspired by the death of John Brown. In both cases his usual attitudes seem to go awry. In the first, for instance, his beloved "actual," which ordinarily he considered to be "fair as a vision or a dream" (*W*, VIII, 477–78), gets treated in the following manner: "I do not think much of the actual. It is something which we have long since done with. It is a sort of vomit in which the unclean love to wallow" (*Ibid.*, 44). And in the entry on John Brown, death forces Thoreau to say: "Beauty stands veiled . . . and music is a screeching lie" (*W*, XVIII, 438). Similarly, on the day of his father's death (February 3, 1858) he noted in his journal:

> I perceive that we partially die ourselves through sympathy at the death of each of our friends or near relatives. Each such experience is an assault on our vital force. It becomes a source of wonder that they who have lost many friends still live. After long watching around the sick-bed of a friend, we, too, partially give up the ghost with him, and are the less to be identified with this state of things. (*W*, XVII, 438)

In the face of death Thoreau loses his ordinarily insatiable appetite for life. Two days later he remarked: "When we have experienced many disappointments, such as the loss of friends, the notes of birds cease to affect us as they did" (*Ibid.*, 439).

Thoreau's treatment of death in his journal, then, is neither optimistic nor triumphant; it often simply amounts to a species of breathless terror, as in the following entries: "Dispose of evil. Get punished once for all. Die, if you can. Depart." And: "Be sure you die. Finish your work. Know when to leave off" (*W*, VIII, 44; XVIII, 438). These passages clearly confirm Perry Miller's observation that where death is concerned, Thoreau "demands the pure process of decomposition, and he wants it over with quickly." [47] He found the thought of death intolerable and therefore wished to dispose of it in haste.

This suggests why, for Thoreau, the notion of death in its worst form was the idea of being buried alive—a prolonged death agony. In fact, this is exactly how the dark theme of extinction finds its way into the optimistic structure of *Walden*—in the shape of Thoreau's excessive dislike of houses. The reader of the journal is prepared for this symbolic equation of house with tomb by Thoreau's literal need constantly to get out into nature: "Must be out-of-doors enough to get experience of wholesome reality, as a ballast to thought and sentiment. Health requires this relaxation, this aimless life. This life in the present" (*W*, X, 409–10). Indoor thoughts are dark thoughts, and it is really the house that he is escaping:

> Staying in the house breeds a sort of insanity always. Every house is in this sense a hospital. A night and a forenoon is as much confinement to those wards as I can stand. I am aware that I recover some sanity which I had lost almost the instant that I come abroad. (*W*, XV, 200).

In *Walden* the theme is broached immediately in the chapter on "Economy":

> . . . if one designs to construct a dwelling-house, it behooves him to exercise a little Yankee shrewdness, lest after all he find himself in a workhouse, a labyrinth without a clue, a museum, an almshouse, a prison, or a splendid mausoleum instead. (*W*, II, 31)

Thoreau then goes on to relate how he once thought of living in a toolbox, six feet by three, and he jocosely recommends this solution to his readers: "Many a man is harassed to death to pay the rent of a larger and more luxurious box who would not have frozen to death in such a box as this" (*Ibid.*, 32). But the solution is no solution at all, and the humor falls uncomfortably flat: he has described his own coffin. One feels that the problem is insoluble; every house is a tomb. Nevertheless, he continues to pretend that he is interested in theories of housing:

> . . . the cost of a thing is the amount of what I will call life which is required to be exchanged for it, immediately or in the long run. . . . It may be guessed that I reduce almost the whole advantage of holding this superfluous property as a fund in store against the future, so far as the individual is concerned, mainly to the defraying of funeral expenses. But perhaps a man is not required to bury himself. (*Ibid.*, 34)

Since a house is a symbol of mortality, it "defrays" the "expenses" of dying by preparing us in advance; and a man is "required to bury himself" simply by living in it, and paying for it, from day to day, thus daily moving himself closer to his doom. But Thoreau wants no part of this:

> We have built for this world a family mansion, and for the next a family tomb. The best works of art are the expression of man's struggle to free himself from this condition, but the effect of our art is merely to make this low state comfortable and that higher state to be forgotten. (*Ibid.*, 41)

Any art which reconciles man to his mortality is "comfortable." Thoreau wants an art which will express "man's struggle to free himself from this condition," an art capable of circumventing mortality—such as his own art, built on a theory of experiencing life to the utmost intensity in the present moment. He therefore adds quickly: ". . . a taste for the beautiful is most cultivated out of doors, where there is no house and no housekeeper" (*Ibid.*, 42). In this connection, it is important to note that Thoreau's apparent criticism of Horatio Greenough's theories of organic architecture (with which, as F. O. Matthiessen has noted, he really did agree [48]) is less a criticism of Greenough than of architecture in general—any kind of house building:

> Much it concerns a man, forsooth, how a few sticks are slanted over him or under him, and what colors are daubed upon his box. It would signify somewhat if, in any earnest sense, *he* slanted them and daubed it; but the spirit having departed out of the tenant, it is of a piece with constructing his own coffin,—the architecture of the grave,—and "carpenter" is but another name for "coffin-maker." One man says, in his despair or indifference to life, take up a handful of the earth at your feet, and paint your house that color. Is he thinking of his last and narrow house? (*Ibid.*, 53)

A house is always a tomb, and Thoreau solves his architectural quandary by avoiding houses and living outdoors as much as possible.

The great difficulty for Thoreau was that he had discovered evil in the fabric of nature in the form of decay and death, and it was impossible for him to accommodate this evil in his theories; indeed, it was the very negation of all his theories. Moreover, he had a constant *memento mori* in front of his eyes and nose in the shape of the fungus, which represented for him all that was ugly and malevolent in the world. In his journal, "the Pyramids and other monuments of Egypt are a vast mildew or toadstools"; a priest is "the fungus of the graveyard, the mildew of the tomb"; the life of an alcoholic "is like that of a fungus"; and even cowards are referred to as "fungi" (*W*, XV, 274–75; XVIII, 378, 438). For Thoreau an actual fungus was always, like death, a puzzle and a horror; and in this, as in so many other respects, the difference between Thoreau and

Emerson is patent. When Emerson, in his journal for 1838, records his encounter with a fungus, the conclusion he draws is simply that it proves "there is comedy in the Divine Mind" (J, V, 53–54). As with death, Emerson absorbs the fungus into his optimistic cosmic scheme. For Thoreau the lesson of the fungus is much darker; if it exhibits cosmic humor, it is no better than the humor of the "jakes" (W, IX, 255). But Thoreau does not really find the fungus comic; it is "in all respects a most disgusting object" (W, XV, 116). And in a long and fascinating journal passage on the *phallus impudicus,* Thoreau—seemingly driven by the imp of the perverse—forces himself to examine carefully the ultimate horror in nature, as if he were willfully and terribly toying with the idea of death: [49]

> It was as offensive to the eye as to the scent, the cap rapidly melting and defiling what it touched with a fetid, olivaceous, semiliquid matter. In an hour or two the plant scented the whole house wherever placed, so that it could not be endured. I was afraid to sleep in my chamber where it had lain until the room had been well ventilated. It smelled like a dead rat in the ceiling, in all the ceilings of the house. Pray, what was Nature thinking of when she made this? She almost puts herself on a level with those who draw in privies. (*Ibid.,* 117)

The question goes unanswered, and the only solution, apparently, is to avoid the fungus.

Thoreau's aching need to escape both houses and fungi—at once emblems and embodiments of mortality—is finally expressed in *Walden* by his twisted description of a "model farm":

> Farmers are respectable and interesting to me in proportion as they are poor,—poor farmers. A model farm! where the house stands like a fungus in a muck-heap, chambers for men, horses, oxen, and swine, cleansed and uncleansed, all contiguous to

one another! Stocked with men! A great grease-spot, redolent of manures and buttermilk! Under a high state of cultivation, being manured with the hearts and brains of men! As if you were to raise your potatoes in the churchyard! Such is a model farm. (*W*, II, 218)

One might as well live in a graveyard as live on a farm—or in any house, for that matter. Thoreau can only hope that the place he has chosen for his gardening is free of the taint of mortality: "I am not aware that any man has ever built on the spot which I occupy. Deliver me from a city built on the site of a more ancient city, whose materials are ruins, whose gardens cemetaries" (*Ibid.*, 291). But, of course, there is finally no escape; and at the end of *Walden* Thoreau can do nothing but attempt (in Perry Miller's phrase) to "elude death's cosmic conspiracy" [50] by miraculously transforming the grave into a cradle and declaring that the tomb is in reality a chrysalis:

Who knows what beautiful and winged life, whose egg has been buried for ages under many concentric layers of wooden-ness in the dead dry life of society, deposited at first in the alburnum of the green and living tree, which has been gradually converted into the semblance of its well-seasoned tomb,—heard perchance gnawing out now for years by the astonished family of man, as they sat round the festive board,—may unexpectedly come forth from amidst society's most trivial and handselled furniture, to enjoy its perfect summer life at last! (*W*, II, 367)

The boast is exhilarating, and Thoreau's triumph in *Walden* is imaginatively complete for most readers. But we must still notice that although "there is more day to dawn" (*Ibid.*), Thoreau himself has taught only too well that morning is the time of youth (*W*, XI, 393). "Remember thy Creator in the days of thy youth," he wrote in 1851. "Sing while you may, before the evil days come. . . . See, hear, smell, taste, etc., while these senses are fresh and pure" (*W*, VIII, 330). For inexorably, as Thoreau knew and feared, "the night cometh, when no man can work." [51] Thoreau's theory of art—in Pater's phrase, a "desperate effort to see and touch"—is a theory built on the illusory hope of perennial youth and in frantic defiance of the exigencies of age.

··ɔ[CHAPTER SEVEN]ɔ··

Conclusion

All intellectual virtue consists in a reliance on Ideas. It must be carried with a certain magnificence. We must live by our strength, not by our weakness. . . . Why should we be the dupes of our senses, the victims of our own works, and always inferior to ourselves. We do not yet trust the unknown powers of thought. . . . The world is intellectual; and the man is.

Emerson, "The Natural History of Intellect"

*   *   *

A man may be old and infirm. What, then, are the thoughts he thinks? what the life he lives? They and it are, like himself, infirm. But a man may be young, athletic, active, beautiful. Then, too, his thoughts will be like his person. They will wander in a living and beautiful world. If you are well, then how brave you are! How you hope! You are conversant with joy! A man thinks as well through his legs and arms as his brain. We exaggerate the importance and exclusiveness of the headquarters.

Thoreau, *Journal,* December 31, 1859

*   *   *

IF the basis of Emerson's thought and art (the moral law) is imaginatively insufficient, we might say that the foundation of

Thoreau's art (momentary ecstasy and epiphany reached through the senses) is teleologically inadequate. But taken together, the two theories represent the major impulses—ethical and ecstatic—behind the attempt of the Transcendentalists to go beyond what they considered the traditional forms and categories of experience. Renewal was the essential goal of Transcendentalism—the hope of establishing, in Emerson's phrase, "an original relation to the universe" (C, I, 3). The primary task of Transcendentalism, therefore, became an exploration of the self and nature.

To define succinctly the difference between the Transcendentalism of Emerson and that of Thoreau, one might say that Emerson found man and the natural world instinct with law and that Thoreau found them instinct with sensibility. In a brilliant sentence, Santayana once noted "how metaphysical was the passion that drove the Puritans to [these] shores." [1] As Transcendentalists, Emerson and Thoreau exemplify the two elements—metaphysical and passional—which Santayana considered primal in the American spirit. Any adequate definition of Transcendentalism must deal with both impulses—must, in short, face the difficult task of reconciling Emerson and Thoreau, refractory in their lives but complementary in their thought.

It is a truism, but a helpful one to remember, that Emerson was essentially a Protestant for whom Christianity was valuable as a perfect guide to conduct but not as an object of literal belief. In the manner of the rationalist critics of his age, Emerson considered Christ not the actual Messiah, but simply a great ethical teacher; the notion of God's really assuming the flesh or of man's carnal apotheosis seemed to him unworthy of belief and unnecessary for true religion. It is useful to turn to Emerson's farewell sermon to the Second Church in Boston, "The Lord's Supper" (1832), as a reminder of just how vigorous a part he played in the liberalizing and rationalizing movements characteristic of nineteenth-century Protestantism. In the relentless logic of its organization, the equanimity of its temper, and the perfect clarity of its tone and diction, the sermon is undoubtedly among the best things Emerson ever wrote. One suspects that he put a great deal of himself into it.

Emerson's major objection to the Eucharist lay in the fact that he found it historically unjustified and unjustifiable. What is more revealing for our purposes, he thought it totally unnecessary for the practice of Christianity:

> We are not accustomed to express our thoughts or emotions by symbolical actions. Most men find the bread and wine no aid to devotion, and to some it is a painful impediment. To eat bread is one thing; to love the precepts of Christ and resolve to obey them is quite another. (C, XI, 19)

Several basic Emersonian attitudes are expressed in this passage. But first, a question of simple paradox presents itself. How could the same Emerson who denied the importance of "symbolical actions" in 1832 publish four years later a great manifesto declaring that nature is the "symbolical action" *par excellence* of man's mind? The answer is, as we have already noted, that the highly idealistic thesis of *Nature*—Emerson's insistence that the world exists to symbolize man's ethical (divine) impulse—was meant simply as a figure of speech in an argument for right conduct. Emerson tried to emphasize the importance of conduct, not of symbolization. Implicitly convinced of his own "thoughts," he apparently did not consider that through participation in a "symbolical action" a man might actually come to believe actively in an ideal that had been previously just that and nothing more. It is, of course, an idea very old in Christian thought that the *act* of faith must precede the intellectual *awareness* of faith. Emerson's assertion that "most men find the bread and wine no aid to devotion" shows to what extent, limited by his own austere tastes and his sense of not needing any "aid," he could cause himself to forget the long history of Christian devotion.

To be sure, in his essay "Country Life" (1858), Emerson noted that "the gulf between our seeing and our doing is a symbol of that between faith and experience" (*C*, XII, 157), complaining thereby that our faith in the existence of nature's "angelic radiations" (*Ibid.*) by no means guarantees our ability actively to recreate or participate in the experience—truly to *believe* in it. He perceived the "gulf" but sadly considered it unbreachable, since, with his habitual disdain for experience, he had always found the actual hopelessly inferior to his ideal: "To eat bread is one thing; to love the precepts of Christ and resolve to obey them is quite another." Convinced of the eternal disparity in value between bread and truth, he did not really believe that man could find God in the very act of eating, in the consecration of the carnal; nor, apparently, did he stop to consider that a man might cease to love the precepts of Christ if he could not find them present to the senses in his very bread.

Thoreau, like Emerson, was by descent and temperament also a Protestant (though scarcely a Christian), yet no mere religious differences could blind him to the essential truth about an act of communion, as this journal passage implies: "We pluck and eat in remembrance of Her. It is a sacrament, a communion" (*W*, XI, 331). Here Thoreau's "bread and wine" is the huckleberry, his union is with nature, and there is no question of resolving to obey precepts. "Slight and innocent savors, which relate us to Nature," he goes on, "make us her guests and entitle us to her regard and protection." Thoreau's performance of this act leads to nature's "regard"—the real experience of her "angelic radiations." Communion is then a ritual, a "symbolical action," participation in which carries one to the actual sense of faith.

As a recent critic of Thoreau points out, "Thoreau patterns

his actions far more than most other Transcendentalists: he does not overthrow, but rather establishes anew, ritual, celebration, holiday." [2] Thoreau recognized the importance of concrete ceremonial because, as we have seen, he believed that religious experience was coterminous with the experience of the body and that he could make neither life nor art out of an abstraction.[3] Even Carlyle, with all his sympathy for Emerson's aims and principles, never tired of castigating his friend for his refusal to embrace experience in his writings: "Surely I could wish you *returned* into your own poor nineteenth-century . . . and trying to evolve in some measure the hidden Godlike that lies in *it;*—that seems to me the kind of feat for literary men." [4] Carlyle could take Emerson to task for his abstractions in a positively Thoreauvian voice:

> All theory becomes more and more confessedly inadequate, untrue, unsatisfactory, almost a kind of mockery to me! I will have all things condense themselves, take shape and body, if they are to have my sympathy. I have a *body* myself; in the brown leaf, sport of the Autumn wind, I find what mocks all prophesyings, even Hebrew ones . . .[5]

Carlyle asked his friend for exactly the thing that Emerson had denigrated in "The Lord's Supper"—a symbolical action: "You *tell* us with piercing emphasis that man's soul is great; *show* us a great soul of a man, in some work symbolic of such." [6] Thoreau's experiment at Walden, of course, was precisely this kind of symbolical action: an actual attempt, by participating in the ritual of nature, "to live deep and suck out all the marrow of life" (*W*, II, 101) and thereby, through the concrete, to arrive at the sublime.

Because he was always convinced of the rightness and nobility of a life lived in conformity only to the highest dictates of the conscience, Emerson never ceased trying to instruct his readers in the dangers of fleshly subversion: "Why should we be the dupes of our senses . . ." (C, XII, 80). Thoreau, on the other hand, was certain that a wise man "will confine the observations of his mind as closely as possible to the experience or life of his senses. His thought must live with and be inspired with the life of the body" (W, XI, 16–17).

Emerson felt it was imperative, for the sake of eternity, to subordinate the passions to the will: "The one serious and formidable thing in nature is a will" (C, VI, 30). Thoreau considered this a guarantee of eternal death: "Some men endeavor to live a constrained life, to subject their whole lives to their wills, as he who said he would give a sign if he were conscious after his head was cut off,—but he gave no sign" (W, XI, 17).

Thoreau's question to his generation stressed the importance of sensuous existence: "Will you live? or will you be embalmed?" [7] The elder Transcendentalist, however, perpetually distrustful of forms, including his body, recommended as remedy to his audience of Harvard Divinity students: "first, soul, and second, soul, and evermore, soul" (C, I, 150).

Rapt to a kind of ecstasy by the pure idea of man's soul, Emerson preached as always the sufficiency of the moral law. But Thoreau warned his friend Blake not to trust such a notion: "Do not be too moral. You may cheat yourself out of much life so." [8]

Matthew Arnold once told an American audience that Emerson was our Cardinal Newman and, likening Emerson to Marcus Aurelius, went on to utter a now familiar sentence about the American sage: "He is the friend and aider of those who would live in the spirit." [9] Arnold's juxtaposition of names is highly suggestive: the links of association are disillusionment, a chastened attitude toward life, and the awareness that our only wisdom lies in resigning ourselves both to the evanescence of joy and to the consequent necessity to live only in the mind. Arnold meant that Emerson is the "aider of those who would live in the spirit" because he preached that the only true happiness lies in the spiritual life. In Arnold's words, Emerson's gospel was "Happiness in labour, righteousness, and veracity." [10]

Carlyle, Arnold insisted, was a false teacher, because although he too praised a life of "labour, righteousness, and veracity," he offered as the reward of such a life only dignity, not happiness. Even the common people know better, Arnold argues; and he relates that he was not surprised, when inspecting a school one day, to find:

> . . . the children [were] reading a piece of poetry on the common theme that we are here to-day and gone to-morrow. I shall soon be gone, the speaker in this poem was made to say,—
> > 'And I shall be glad to go,
> > For the world at best is a dreary place,
> > And my life is getting low.' [11]

The people are not distressed by this disparagement of happiness, Arnold says, because they know that in missing out on happiness here below they can still look to it in the hereafter. They are not, at any rate, insofar as they believe in their "popular religion," cheated entirely out of their expected reward. Arnold found Emerson's gospel much more inspiriting, much more hopeful. But, interestingly, the three lines of verse that he quotes read—in theme, anyhow—like a doggerel version of Emerson's "Threnody," that magnificent testament of stoic cosmic consolation. One wonders, in any case, whether *happiness* is quite the word to describe the guerdon of "labour, righteousness, and veracity." Arnold thought so; but then, he seems to have had a temperament very like Emerson's.

Looked at more sympathetically, however, Emerson's gospel unquestionably possesses a certain kind of wisdom. If, as

Thoreau so tirelessly insisted, the only real joy is of the body
and we should therefore "dwell as near as possible to the
channel in which . . . life flows" (W, XI, 17)—the
senses—would not the ever-threatening loss of physical vitality
represent a true occasion for tragedy? One does not have to
read very far in Emerson to notice that this was a familiar line
of reasoning for him and to learn what his solution was: "In
phlegmatic natures calamity is unaffecting" (C, XII, 410).
Emerson's denial of the body, his erection of the will at the
expense of passional life, was a conscious attempt to forestall
calamity. Accordingly, the real theme of his essay on "The
Tragic" is that he who would avoid danger must practice
detachment: "We must walk as guests in Nature; not impassioned, but cool and disengaged" (Ibid., 413). He therefore
cautioned that a man "should keep as much as possible the
reins in his own hands, rarely giving way to extreme emotion of
joy or grief" (Ibid., 411).

Arnold's version of Emerson implies just this sort of analysis. A life devoted to virtue is happier than one predicated on
emotional satisfaction because pleasure and pain are close
relations: one gives up great joy to avoid the possibility of
great anguish. Emerson is "the friend and aider of those who
would live in the spirit" because he points out the stoic way to
this attenuated but unassailable happiness, as the conclusion
of "The Tragic" makes clear:

> . . . higher still than the activities of art, the intellect in its
> purity and the moral sense in its purity are not distinguished
> from each other, and both ravish us into a region whereunto
> these passionate clouds of sorrow cannot rise. (Ibid., 417)

Sorrow and pain cannot follow the man who has resolutely
turned away from his feelings and found refuge in the mind.
We get beyond tragedy by transcending our emotions.[12]
But there is more to Emerson's stratagem—in fact, a sober

attempt to deal with the problem of death. For if death is the end of feeling and of joy, it is obviously a tragic fact for someone in love with the ecstasy of being; and there is no way to avoid the difficulty except by learning to give up early what we must relinquish eventually. "The only way to become acquainted with death," says Montaigne, "is to approach it." In a manner of speaking, we may say that we can only learn to die by ceasing beforehand to live completely—by considering life as a preparation for death. There is, then, a kind of teleology implied in Emerson's dogged insistence on the necessary supremacy of the life of the mind. By a persistent denial of the flesh, he hoped to ensure his body's acquiescence to the ultimate triumph of the soul—for Emerson, the primary entelechy of being.

Edgar Allan Poe once noted that in discussions of Transcendentalism one should avoid at all costs "the Infernal Twoness." [13] For our purposes it is in fact very helpful to think of both Emerson and Thoreau as indefatigable monists. Despite an occasional struggle over the dualism of mind and body, Emerson tended to insist, metaphorically or otherwise, that only spirit exists. Death thereby loses its sting. For Thoreau the problem of dualism is solved by an association of spiritual life with the life of the body—that is, only body exists. This leaves death as an inescapable fact, and death was the one fact that Thoreau had trouble "translating" in his usual fashion (cf. *W*, IX, 311). Emerson's solution was no solution at all for Thoreau because he could never relinquish his belief in the primacy of sense experience.

Interestingly, the problem with which Thoreau found himself confronted as a result of his beliefs has a striking affinity to matters discussed by Freud in *Beyond the Pleasure Principle*. In this late work Freud modified his earlier theories by postulating "the activity of . . . two instinctual impulses, the life instincts and the death instincts." [14] In the course of a discussion of the meaning of "instincts," Freud theorized that the "instinctual" is related to what he called the "compulsion to repeat," a compulsion that goes beyond the "pleasure principle" because it represents an instinctual urge in man to return to quiescence—non-being or death. Freud then related this "compulsion to repeat"—the urge to death—to certain cyclical processes in natural and animal life.[15]

Thoreau's obsessive concern with the cycle of nature seems to be very clearly related to Freud's formulation. Thoreau, as we have noted, tried to convince himself that by associating with the perennial return of life, he could triumph over death. But it is not even necessary for us to invoke the Freudian principle of the "affirmation of the opposite" (so familiar in dream interpretation) to recognize that Thoreau found the opposite lesson embodied in the revolution of the seasons. He tells us himself that nature is not only reborn but also dies each year, leaving us perplexed to know *what*, in fact, we have been taught.[16] In Thoreau's writings, that is, the death instincts—as well as the life instincts—are expressed in the metaphor of the eternal return of the seasons. For Thoreau's major purpose, the metaphor fails of complete success because, although he wished it to symbolize his cyclical participation in rebirth, it also stands, paradoxically, for the very opposite.

Nor are we left with only half of Freud's theory, for the "sexual instinct"—"the embodiment of the will to live" [17]—is at the very heart of Thoreau's writings. The perceptive reader has never been fooled by Thoreau's apparent fastidiousness into believing that sexuality was not present, nor should the modern reader be misled by recent critical cries of "incipient homosexuality." [18] The deeper truth, as Norman O. Brown has ably demonstrated, is that the fullest sexuality can only be defined by the term that Freud applied to infants, whom he called "polymorphously perverse," since their whole body is a zone of pleasure. The infant's laudable aim, as Brown suggests, is to unite with the world in love and pleasure.[19] And this is fundamentally what Thoreau's mystic quest was about.

Brown's optimistic conclusion is that when the fullest and healthiest expression of Eros is achieved, death will cease to be a problem: "The death instinct is reconciled with the life instinct only in a life which is not repressed, which leaves no 'unlived lines' in the human body, the death instinct then being affirmed in a body which is willing to die." [20] Thoreau, unfortunately, like Freud after him, was unable to achieve such a synthesis.[21] Left with two principles—passional energy and death—he lived his life as a tragic struggle in which, besides death, nothing was certain but his momentary ecstasies, at once glorious and terrible: "The thrills of joy and those of pain," he noted on an exquisite day in September, "are indistinguishable." [22]

Notes

Chapter One: *Introduction*

1. Mark Van Doren, *Henry David Thoreau* (Boston: Houghton Mifflin, 1916), pp. 70, 91.

2. *The Complete Writings of Nathaniel Hawthorne,* Old Manse Edition (Boston and New York, 1900), IV, xx.

3. Quoted in Ralph L. Rusk, *The Life of Ralph Waldo Emerson* (New York: Columbia University Press, 1957), pp. 286–87.

4. Compare, for example, *The Correspondence of Henry David Thoreau,* ed. Walter Harding and Carl Bode (New York: New York University Press, 1958), pp. 29–30, where the editors allow themselves to say that "the Transcendentalists were well agreed that . . . knowledge from within was superior to, and transcended, any knowledge gained from without." In the first place, such a statement can only make us feel that those quaint nineteenth-century Concordians, blessed innocents dwelling in a private world of perfect faith, have absolutely nothing to say to us victims of the twentieth century, too harried almost to believe in our own existence and surrounded as we are by a world so appallingly real that exclusive dependence on "knowledge from within" would threaten death at every street corner. But, as a matter of fact, assuming that the statement as offered would have had meaning for any Transcendentalist, Emerson and Thoreau were certainly *not* "well agreed" on this point.

5. Rusk, *op. cit.,* pp. 372–73.

6. Octavius B. Frothingham, *Transcendentalism in New England* (New York, 1876), p. 111.

7. Cf. also George Ripley and Theodore Parker, in Perry Miller, *The Transcendentalists* (Cambridge: Harvard University Press, 1950), especially pp. 139, 263, 277.

8. Frothingham, *op. cit.*, p. 227.

9. Harold Clarke Goddard, *Studies in New England Transcendentalism* (New York, 1908), p. 9.

10. Quoted in *ibid.*, pp. 58–59.

11. *Ibid.*, p. 78.

12. *Ibid.*, p. 130.

13. *Ibid.*, p. 191.

14. *Ibid.*, p. 192.

15. Goddard's distinction seems to me a fair and useful one, although I do not mean to imply that Emerson can in no way be considered a mystic. Indeed, the question of Emerson's "mysticism" has stimulated a good deal of critical discussion and, in a certain sense, is probably not resolvable; it simply depends on one's definitions. To cite two examples, one on either side: Frederic I. Carpenter, in his *Emerson Handbook* (New York: Hendricks House, 1953), claims that Emerson was a mystic of the Western, "dynamic" kind; "for Emerson, the mystical experience was dynamically a means, rather than passively an end, and the goal of mysticism was insight into the active conduct of life" (p. 115). Patrick Quinn, in "Emerson and Mysticism" (*American Literature*, XXI [January 1950], 397–414), rejects Emerson's mysticism on this very basis, by distinguishing between "the mystic and the humanist. The former is concerned primarily with God; the latter is concerned exclusively with man" (p. 400). Quinn argues, I think correctly, that Emerson's "mystical experience" always ends in ethics and not in union with God. However, Quinn's denial that "nature ecstasy" constitutes a true mystical experience leaves the latter too narrowly defined. It seems to me that the "illuminated moment," sought as an end in itself, has every right to be called "mystical," whether it be reached in a monastery, in the woods, or in a subway train. Certainly much of the literature, especially the poetry, of the Western world in the nineteenth and twentieth centuries assumes that the "mystical experience" can occur in commonplace situations.

16. In Miller, *op. cit.*, p. 435.

17. Arthur O. Lovejoy, *The Great Chain of Being* (Cambridge: Harvard University Press, 1936), p. 244.

18. Cf. Rusk, *op. cit.*, p. 160.

19. Insofar as Emersonian "Compensation" is a justification of misfortune, it is implied in the principle of "Plentitude": since the Chain of Being is complete, it must include all possible existences ("All must full or not coherent be,/And all that rises, rise in due degree"), and this includes "evil" or "deprived" creatures. Lovejoy quotes Soame Jenyns on this point: "I am persuaded that there is something in the abstract nature of pain conducive to pleasure; that the sufferings of individuals are absolutely necessary to universal happiness. . . . Scarce one instance, I believe, can be produced of the acquisition of pleasure or convenience by any creatures, which is not purchased by the previous or consequential sufferings of themselves or others." (*Op. cit.*, p. 209.) Cf. *Jn*, I, 187.

20. Lovejoy, *op. cit.*, p. 89.

21. Cf. Perry Miller, *The New England Mind* (New York: Macmillan), I (1939), 213–14; and *The Letters of Ralph Waldo Emerson*, ed. Ralph L. Rusk (New York: Columbia University Press, 1939), I, 84–85.

22. Cf. *The Works of George Santayana*, Triton Edition (New York: Scribner's), VII (1937), 215.

Chapter Two: *Emerson: The Artist of the Prudential*

1. *The Complete Writings of Nathaniel Hawthorne*, Old Manse Edition (Boston and New York, 1900), V, 229. Hawthorne reproduced this situation in "The Custom House," the prefatory sketch to *The Scarlet Letter*. There the three estates are represented by the "Custom House," Ticonderoga (the "Old General"), and the "Old Inspector." Hawthorne is once again the outsider, the spectator. And, as in "Passages," he is reviled by his Puritan ancestors for being a wastrel and an idler (*ibid.*, VI, 11–12).

2. *Ibid.*, V, 232.

3. *Ibid.*, p. 250.

4. *Ibid.*, p. 252.

5. *Ibid.*, p. 234.

6. *Ibid.*, XVII, 293.

7. *Ibid.*, II, 96.

8. *Ibid.*, pp. 94–95.

9. *Ibid.*, p. 96.

10. *Ibid.*, XVII, 298.

11. *Ibid.*, pp. 312–13.

12. Ralph L. Rusk, *The Life of Ralph Waldo Emerson* (New York: Columbia University Press, 1957), p. 405.

13. Hawthorne, *op. cit.*, II, 301.

14. *Ibid.*, p. 305.

15. *Ibid.*, p. 304.

16. In Perry Miller, *The Transcendentalists* (Cambridge: Harvard University Press, 1950), p. 432.

17. *Ibid.*, pp. 433–34.

18. *J*, III, 186. Cf. Emerson on Goethe in *The Correspondence of Thomas Carlyle and Ralph Waldo Emerson*, ed. C. E. Norton (Boston, 1883), I, 30–31.

19. Thomas Shepard, quoted in Kenneth Murdock, *Literature and Theology in Colonial New England* (Cambridge: Harvard University Press, 1949), p. 62.

20. Thomas Mann, *Doctor Faustus*, trans. H. T. Lowe-Porter (New York: Alfred A. Knopf, 1948), p. 490.

21. Hawthorne, *op. cit.*, III, 245.

22. *Ibid.*, p. 246.

23. Perry Miller, *Consciousness in Concord* (Boston: Houghton Mifflin, 1958), pp. 119–21.

24. See *The Letters of Ralph Waldo Emerson*, ed. Ralph L. Rusk (New York: Columbia University Press, 1939), III, 172.

25. *Ibid.*, IV, 151.

26. *Ibid.*

27. *The Correspondence of Henry David Thoreau*, ed. Walter Harding and Carl Bode (New York: New York University Press, 1958), pp. 249–50. Cf. Miller, *Consciousness in Concord*, pp. 36–38.

28. Hawthorne, *op. cit.*, XVIII, 297.
29. *J*, V, 192. Cf. Thoreau: "As to conforming outwardly, and living your own life inwardly, I have not a very high opinion of that course. Do not let your right hand know what your left hand does in that line of business. I have no doubt it will prove a failure" (*W*, VIII, 48).
30. In Miller, *The Transcendentalists*, p. 58.
31. *J*, VIII, 424. Cf. Thoreau, *W*, XVII, 326–29.

Chapter Three: *Nature as Symbol: Emerson's Noble Doubt*

1. *C*, III, 51. Cf. Emerson himself on Plotinus in his "Thoreau," *C*, X, 461.
2. *J*, VI, 447. Cf. Ralph L. Rusk, *The Life of Ralph Waldo Emerson* (New York: Columbia University Press, 1957), p. 358.
3. Quoted in Rusk, *op. cit.*, p. 301. It is instructive to compare Emerson's letter to Carlyle on this occasion with Carlyle's response; see *The Correspondence of Thomas Carlyle and Ralph Waldo Emerson*, ed. C. E. Norton (Boston, 1883), I, 357–65.
4. Rusk, *op. cit.*, p. 301.
5. See *The Letters of Ralph Waldo Emerson*, ed. Ralph L. Rusk (New York: Columbia University Press, 1939), III, 4.
6. Rusk, *Life*, p. 150.
7. *W*, VII, 303. Cf. another statement by Thoreau: "I don't like people who are too good for this world. Let a man reserve a good appetite for his peck of dirt, and expect his chief wealth in unwashed diamonds. To know nature and ourselves well, we must have acquired a certain hardness and habitual equanimity.

"The virtue of some is only an excessive refinement." (In Perry Miller, *Consciousness in Concord* [Boston: Houghton Mifflin, 1958], p. 211.)
8. *J*, V, 485. Cf. Carlyle's remark to Emerson: "What a view must a man have of this Universe, who thinks 'he can swallow it all,' who is not doubly and trebly happy that he can keep it from swallowing him!" (Carlyle and Emerson, *Correspondence*, II, 18.)

9. *The Works of George Santayana,* Triton Edition (New York: Scribner's), II (1936), 154.

10. Richard Price, *A Review of the Principal Questions and Difficulties in Morals* (2nd ed.; London, 1769), p. 150.

11. Price, *op. cit.,* p. 169.

12. See especially C, I, 50–51. For a discussion of the particular fallacy which Emerson employs here (and of the problems of dualism in general), see Arthur O. Lovejoy, *The Revolt Against Dualism* (LaSalle, Illinois: Open Court, W. W. Norton, 1930), pp. 48–49.

13. Of course, as Arthur Lovejoy has pointed out in his learned discussion of the many confusions in the use of the term *Romanticism* ("On the Discrimination of Romanticisms," in *Essays in the History of Ideas* [New York: George Braziller, 1955]), there is also an historically valid use of the word which we might apply to Emerson here, the so-called anti-naturalistic Romanticism. But since we are most familiar with naturalistic Romanticism, one of whose tenets was that man is "naturally" good and therefore needs no conscience, it seems to me fair enough to call attention to the paradox of Emerson's being considered a Romantic. Ultimately, the greater paradox presents itself that after reading Professor Lovejoy's essay, one would feel justified in calling both Rousseau *and* Irving Babbitt Romantics!

14. For this comparison I have drawn heavily upon Perry Miller's interpretations of Edwards, especially in *Jonathan Edwards* (New York: William Sloan, 1949) and in *Images or Shadows of Divine Things* (New Haven: Yale University Press, 1948), pp. 1–41.

15. Miller, *Images,* p. 36.

16. Cf. Edwards: "We can conceive of nothing more beautiful of an external kind than the beauties of nature here, especially the beauty of the more animated parts of this world. We never could have conceived of these if we had not seen them; and now, we can think of nothing beyond them; and therefore the highest beauties of art consist in imitation of them." (Quoted in Miller, *Images,* p. 35.)

Chapter Four: *The Moral Law: Emerson's Cosmic Vision*

1. *The Letters of Ralph Waldo Emerson,* ed. Ralph L. Rusk (New York: Columbia University Press, 1939), II, 397.
2. Ralph L. Rusk, *The Life of Ralph Waldo Emerson* (New York: Columbia University Press, 1957), p. 82.
3. Merrell R. Davis, "Emerson's 'Reason' and the Scottish Philosophers," *New England Quarterly,* XVII (June 1944), 218–19.
4. Leslie Stephen, *History of English Thought in the Eighteenth Century* (New York: G. P. Putnam's, 1927), I, 429. For a sympathetic modern treatment of Price, see Carl B. Cone, *Torchbearer of Freedom* (Lexington: University of Kentucky Press, 1952), especially pp. 20–25 on Price's moral philosophy.
5. *Jn,* I, 334. Cf. *J,* II, 30, where Emerson quotes Aunt Mary on Price: "so eminent, yet so flouted. . . ."
6. Richard Price, *A Review of the Principal Questions and Difficulties in Morals* (2nd ed.; London, 1769), p. 73.
7. *Ibid.,* p. 58.
8. *Ibid.,* p. 23.
9. *Ibid.,* pp. 95–96.
10. See James Bonar, *Moral Sense* (New York: The Macmillan Co., 1930), Chapter III, especially pp. 72–74.
11. Price, *op. cit.,* p. 93.
12. *Ibid.,* p. 140.
13. *Ibid.,* p. 141.
14. *Ibid.,* p. 143.
15. Cf. *ibid.,* pp. 286–88.
16. In Perry Miller, *The Transcendentalists* (Cambridge: Harvard University Press, 1950), p. 54.
17. George Ripley, *Discourses,* in *ibid.,* p. 138.
18. Price, *op. cit.,* p. 283.
19. *Ibid.,* p. 289.
20. *Ibid.,* pp. 73, 78.

21. Yvor Winters, *In Defense of Reason* (Denver: University of Denver Press), pp. 262–82, 577–603.

22. See *The Puritans*, ed. Perry Miller and Thomas H. Johnson (New York: American Book Co., 1938), p. 207.

23. Stephen, *op. cit.*, II, 82–83.

24. Stephen, *op. cit.*, I, 100.

25. Cf. Miller, *The Transcendentalists*, pp. 26–30.

26. "The man of Locke is virtuous without enthusiasm, and intelligent without poetry." (*The Early Lectures of Ralph Waldo Emerson*, ed. Stephen E. Whicher and Robert E. Spiller [Cambridge: Harvard University Press], I [1959], 149.)

27. Cf. William Ellery Channing: ". . . I read Price when I was in college. Price saved me from Locke's Philosophy. He gave me the doctrine of ideas, and during my life I have written the words Love, Right, etc., with a capital. His book, probably, moulded my philosophy into the form it has always retained, and opened my mind into the *transcendental depth*." (Quoted in Harold Clarke Goddard, *Studies in New England Transcendentalism* [New York, 1908], p. 46.)

28. In Miller, *The Transcendentalists*, pp. 47–48.

29. William Henry Channing, quoted in Goddard, *op. cit.*, p. 51.

30. Emerson, *Letters*, I, 412–13.

31. Samuel Taylor Coleridge, *Aids to Reflection* (Burlington, 1829), p. 137.

32. Perhaps even more eagerly because of Milton's apparent sanction of the distinction. Milton's discussion of the matter, as Professor Rusk points out (Emerson, *Letters*, I, 412), was undoubtedly brought to Emerson's attention by James Marsh's quotation from *Paradise Lost* (V, 486–88) in his Preliminary Essay to Coleridge's book. But it has not, I think, been noticed that by quoting out of context, Marsh distorted Milton's meaning. Marsh gives simply the following: "*Fancy* and *understanding*, whence the soul/REASON receives. And reason is her *being*,/ Discursive or intuitive." But Milton adds (in the words of Raphael): "discourse/Is oftest yours, the latter most is ours,/Differing but in degree, of kind the same." That is, discursive reason

(Understanding), which is what men have, differs only in degree from intuitive reason (Reason), which belongs to angels. Emerson's and Coleridge's distinction thus collapses; and Locke, with his pedestrian "Understanding," would seem to have as fair a chance as any Transcendentalist to reach "angelic" knowledge.

33. Arthur O. Lovejoy, "Coleridge and Kant's Two Worlds," *Essays in the History of Ideas* (New York: George Braziller, 1955), pp. 254–76.

34. *The Cambridge History of English Literature*, ed. Sir A. W. Ward and A. R. Waller (Cambridge: Cambridge University Press, 1914), XI, 151–52; noted by Rusk in Emerson, *Letters*, I, 412.

35. Coleridge, *op. cit.*, p. 137.

36. Arthur O. Lovejoy, *The Reason, the Understanding, and Time* (Baltimore: Johns Hopkins Press, 1961), Chapter I, especially pp. 13–15.

37. *Ibid.*, pp. 8–10.

38. René Wellek, "Emerson and German Philosophy," *New England Quarterly*, XVI (1943), 45–46.

39. Madame Germaine de Staël-Holstein, *Germany* (London, 1814), III, 86.

40. *Jn*, I, 377. Emerson also copied into his notebook a skeptical comment on the passage by Thomas Reid, which he apparently ignored: "These . . . are the speculations of men of superior genius; but whether they . . . be as solid as they are sublime; or whether they be the wanderings of imagination, in a region beyond the limits of human understanding, I am unable to determine." (*Ibid.*)

41. *The Works of George Santayana*, Triton Edition (New York: Scribner's), VI (1936), 181.

42. Henry Adams, *The Education of Henry Adams* (New York: Modern Library, 1931), p. 35.

43. John Jay Chapman, *Emerson and Other Essays* (New York, 1898), p. 61.

44. Howard Mumford Jones, "The Influence of European Ideas in Nineteenth-Century America," *American Literature*, VII (1935–36), 262–63.

45. In Perry Miller, *Consciousness in Concord* (Boston: Houghton Mifflin, 1958), p. 210.

46. *W*, VII, 62. Cf. Miller, *Consciousness*, pp. 50–52.

Chapter Five: *Thoreau's Quarrel with the Transcendentalists*

1. *The Correspondence of Henry David Thoreau*, ed. Walter Harding and Carl Bode (New York: New York University Press, 1958), p. 448.

2. *Ibid.*, p. 216.

3. *Ibid.*, p. 444.

4. *Ibid.*, p. 452.

5. *Ibid.*, pp. 283–84.

6. For a scholarly text, notes, and variant readings of this poem, see *Collected Poems of Henry Thoreau*, ed. Carl Bode (Chicago: Packard, 1943), pp. 121–23, 308–9, 358.

7. Thoreau, *Correspondence*, p. 162. As the editors point out (p. 163), F. B. Sanborn suggests that "Teufelsdrock" was Channing himself, and Holbrook Jackson has noted that the "Blumine flower business" refers to Carlyle's *Sartor Resartus*, Chapter V, "Romance."

8. *W*, I, 102. For an excellent discussion of Transcendental poetry in *The Dial*, see Helen Hennessy, "*The Dial*: Its Poetry and Poetic Criticism," *New England Quarterly*, XXXI (March 1958), 66–87.

9. Thoreau, *Collected Poems*, p. 222.

10. Quoted in Thoreau, *Correspondence*, pp. 91–92.

11. *Ibid.*, p. 71.

12. *Ibid.*, p. 154.

13. *Ibid.*, p. 156.

14. *Ibid.*, p. 157.

15. *Ibid.*, p. 200.

16. *Ibid.*, p. 437.

17. *Ibid.*, p. 446.

18. *Ibid.*, p. 447.

19. In Perry Miller, *Consciousness in Concord* (Boston: Houghton Mifflin, 1958), p. 166. Cf. Carlyle's remark to Emerson in *The Correspondence of Thomas Carlyle and Ralph Waldo Emerson*, ed. C. E. Norton (Boston, 1883), I, 314.

20. Thoreau, *Correspondence*, p. 459.

21. *Ibid.*, p. 213.

22. F. O. Matthiessen, *American Renaissance* (New York: Oxford University Press, 1941), p. 92.

23. *The Complete Writings of Nathaniel Hawthorne*, Old Manse Edition (Boston and New York, 1900), IV, 7–8.

24. Thoreau had actually first appeared in print with an obituary in the Concord *Freeman's Gazette* for November 25, 1837. See Walter Harding, *A Thoreau Handbook* (New York: New York University Press, 1959), p. 44.

25. Matthiessen, *loc. cit.* It is also on this point, as I see it, that Andrée Bruel goes wrong in her otherwise excellent work, *Emerson et Thoreau* (Paris, 1929). Her conclusion about Emerson and Thoreau—"Tous deux sont parvenus, avec une démarche différente, à la même conclusion que la nature est un symbole" (p. 181)—simply does not follow from the evidence which she so ably presents.

26. See *The Works of George Santayana*, Triton Edition (New York: Scribner's), II (1936), 192.

27. Thoreau, *Correspondence*, p. 257.

28. *Ibid.*, p. 52.

29. *Ibid.*, p. 70.

30. *Ibid.*, p. 216.

31. Santayana, *op. cit.*, 132.

32. Thoreau, *Correspondence*, pp. 216–17.

Chapter Six: *Thoreau's Aesthetic: A Purely Sensuous Life*

1. *The Correspondence of Henry David Thoreau*, ed. Walter Harding and Carl Bode (New York: New York University Press, 1958), p. 216.

2. *The Letters of Ralph Waldo Emerson,* ed. Ralph L. Rusk (New York: Columbia University Press, 1939), III, 178.

3. *Ibid.,* IV, 376.

4. *The Works of George Santayana,* Triton Edition (New York: Scribner's), VIII (1937), 104.

5. *The Letters of John Keats,* ed. Hyder Rollins (Cambridge: Harvard University Press, 1958), I, 185.

6. Wallace Stevens, *Collected Poems* (New York: Alfred A. Knopf, 1957), p. 64.

7. In referring to Thoreau as a Lockean, I am of course speaking of Locke's epistemology and psychology, not of his ethics. For the dispute over Locke, see Merle Curti, "The Great Mr. Locke: America's Philosopher, 1783–1861," *The Huntington Library Bulletin,* No. 11 (April 1937), 107–51; and Cameron Thompson, "John Locke and New England Transcendentalism," *New England Quarterly,* XXXV (December 1962), 435–57. See also Perry Miller, *The Transcendentalists* (Cambridge: Harvard University Press, 1950), *passim.*

8. Emerson, *Letters,* III, 172.

9. Quoted by Octavius B. Frothingham, *Transcendentalism in New England* (New York, 1876), p. 118.

10. In Perry Miller, *op. cit.,* p. 424.

11. Especially, Shelley in *A Defence of Poetry* and Keats in "Sleep and Poetry."

12. In Perry Miller, *Consciousness in Concord* (Boston: Houghton Mifflin, 1958), p. 191.

13. *Ibid.,* p. 165.

14. *Boswell's Life of Johnson,* ed. G. Birkbeck Hill (Oxford, 1887), IV, 413.

15. See *W,* X, 128, 284–85, 306 ff.; XI, 247, 383; XII, 4; and XIV, 42.

16. Ralph L. Rusk, *The Life of Ralph Waldo Emerson* (New York: Columbia University Press, 1957), p. 435. Cf. Carlyle's remark on Hegel in *The Correspondence of Thomas Carlyle and Ralph Waldo Emerson,* ed. C. E. Norton (Boston, 1883), II, 368–69.

17. Josiah Royce, *The Spirit of Modern Philosophy* (Boston and New York, 1893), p. 209.

18. Cf. Henry Aiken's observation: "Hegel's philosophy of freedom . . . exhibits that paradoxical combination of outward subservience or even servility toward the state and inner spiritual freedom which is so frequently to be found among German intellectuals. Similar traits may also be discerned in such other representatives of Germany's golden age as Leibniz, Goethe, and even Kant. In Hegel's case, it is only fair to say that he regards conformity to the institutionalized duties imposed by society as merely one aspect of self-culture." (*The Age of Ideology* [Boston: Houghton Mifflin, 1957], p. 80.)

19. To James, who here followed Swedenborg, selfhood, or "proprium," was "the source of all evil." (See especially *Society the Redeemed Form of Man*, pp. 484–85.) Despite his agreement with James in his journal, Emerson, in his essay "Greatness" (in *Letters and Social Aims*), writes of Swedenborg's "proprium" as if the latter had considered it a good thing.

20. See Mildred Silver, "Emerson and the Idea of Progress," *American Literature*, XII (March 1940), 1–19. For Emerson and Etzler, see *J*, VII, 271, and *C*, I, 382.

21. Royce, *op. cit.*, p. 207.

22. Cf. *W*, IX, 231: "Obey the spur of the moment. . . . Let the spurs of countless moments goad us incessantly into life. I feel the spur of the moment thrust deep into my side. The present is an inexorable rider."

23. Thoreau, *Correspondence*, p. 222.

24. *Ibid.*, p. 444.

25. *Ibid.*, p. 424.

26. *W*, X, 466–67. Richard Chenevix Trench (1807–86), English divine and philologist, originated the scheme for the Oxford English Dictionary.

27. Thoreau, *Correspondence*, pp. 491–92.

28. *Ibid.*, p. 222.

29. *Ibid.*, pp. 296–97.

30. *Ibid.*, p. 186.

31. Walter Pater, *The Renaissance* (London, 1922), pp. 236–39. Cf. Mark Van Doren, *Henry David Thoreau* (Boston: Houghton Mifflin, 1916), pp. 81–86. For a suggestive discussion of visual "illumination"—adapted, as Pater acknowledges, from Plato's *Phaedrus*—see *Marius the Epicurean*, Chapter III.

32. Bernard Berenson, *Sketch for a Self-Portrait* (New York: Pantheon, 1949), p. 18.

33. Santayana, *op. cit.*, X (1937), 209.

34. *Ibid.*

35. *Ibid.*, II (1936), 162.

36. *Ibid.*, XIV (1937), 170.

37. *Ibid.*, 175–79.

38. *The Letters of George Santayana*, ed. Daniel Cory (New York: Scribner's, 1955), p. 265.

39. Richard Ellmann, *James Joyce* (New York: Oxford University Press, 1959), p. 87. See also James Joyce, *Epiphanies*, ed. O. A. Silverman (Buffalo: University of Buffalo, 1956), especially pp. ix–xvi.

40. Harry Levin, *James Joyce* (Norfolk, Connecticut: New Directions, 1960), pp. 28–29.

41. Henry James, *Partial Portraits* (London and New York, 1888), p. 390.

42. Henry James, *The Portrait of a Lady* (London, 1921), pp. x–xi.

43. Ellmann, *op. cit.*, p. 150.

44. Henry James, *Hawthorne* (New York, 1887), p. 96. But cf. Thoreau's anticipation of this criticism in *W*, IX, 217. Cf. also his justification of his method, *ibid.*, 239.

45. *The Letters of Matthew Arnold to Arthur Hugh Clough*, ed. Howard Foster Lowry (New York: Oxford University Press, 1932), p. 128.

46. Cf. Miller, *Consciousness*, pp. 55–79.

47. *Ibid.*, p. 66.

48. F. O. Matthiessen, *American Renaissance* (New York: Oxford University Press, 1941), pp. 153–57.

49. Cf. Norman O. Brown: "In the last analysis, the peculiar human fascination with excrement is the peculiar human fascina-

tion with death." (*Life Against Death* [Middletown, Conn.: Wesleyan University Press, 1959], p. 295.)

50. Miller, *Consciousness,* p. 79.

51. Cf. Thoreau's pun on a day in "November Eat-heart": "It is but a short time, these afternoons, before the night cometh, in which no man can walk" (*W, XVI, 203). Cf. also *W, IX, 221–22.

Chapter Seven: *Conclusion*

1. *The Works of George Santayana,* Triton Edition (New York: Scribner's), VIII (1937), 7.

2. Paul Lauter, "Thoreau's Prophetic Testimony," *The Massachusetts Review,* IV, No. 1 (Autumn 1962), 117.

3. Cf. *W, IX, 36: "The poet writes the history of his body."

4. *The Correspondence of Thomas Carlyle and Ralph Waldo Emerson,* ed. C. E. Norton (Boston, 1883), II, 11–12.

5. *Ibid.,* I, 304–5.

6. *Ibid.,* 216.

7. *The Correspondence of Henry David Thoreau,* ed. Walter Harding and Carl Bode (New York: New York University Press, 1958), p. 257.

8. *Ibid.,* p. 216.

9. Matthew Arnold, *Discourses in America* (London, 1889), p. 179.

10. *Ibid.,* p. 202.

11. *Ibid.,* p. 201.

12. For a more positive view of Emerson and the tragic sense, see Newton Arvin, "The House of Pain," in *Emerson,* ed. Milton Konvitz and Stephen Whicher (Englewood Cliffs, New Jersey: Prentice-Hall, 1962), pp. 46–59.

13. *The Works of Edgar Allan Poe,* ed. E. C. Stedman and G. E. Woodberry (Chicago: Stone & Kimball, 1894), IV, 205.

14. *The Complete Psychological Works of Sigmund Freud,* translated under the general editorship of James Strachey (London: The Hogarth Press), XVIII (1962), 49.

15. *Ibid.,* pp. 36–37.

16. See Chapter 6, Section vi, above. Cf. e.g., *W*, VIII, 440, and XI, 100.

17. Freud, *op. cit.*, p. 50.

18. See, for example, Carl Bode, "The Half-hidden Thoreau," *The Massachusetts Review*, IV, No. 1 (Autumn 1962), 71. Professor Bode argues that Thoreau willed himself to death because of sexual guilt.

19. Norman O. Brown, *Life Against Death* (Middletown, Conn.: Wesleyan University Press, 1959), Chapter IV, *passim*. Professor Brown's impressive book came into my hands only after the completion of this study, but I was pleased to find in his references to Thoreau an apparent corroboration of my own analysis.

20. *Ibid.*, p. 308.

21. Richard Drinnon, the only other recent critic, besides Norman O. Brown, to suggest the importance of Thoreau's "body mysticism," feels that Thoreau's apparently tranquil death gives proof of just such a synthesis. ("Thoreau's Politics of the Upright Man," *The Massachusetts Review*, IV, No. 1 [Autumn 1962], 137–38.) Every student must decide for himself how to interpret the material, but I am given pause by Thoreau's own remark: "The deathbed scenes and observations even of the best and wisest afford but a sorry picture of our humanity" (*W*, XI, 17).

22. *W*, X, 358. Cf. Brown, *op. cit.*, p. 30.

Index